P9-EDU-882

Toward a Unified Theory of Problem Solving

Views From the Content Domains

Edited by

MIKE U. SMITH

Mercer University School of Medicine

LEA LAWRENCE ERLBAUM ASSOCIATES, PUBLISHERS
1991 Hillsdale, New Jersey   Hove and London

Copyright © 1991 by Lawrence Erlbaum Associates, Inc.
All rights reserved. No part of this book may be reproduced in
any form, by photostat, microform, retrieval system, or any
other means, without the prior written permission of the publisher.

Lawrence Erlbaum, Associates, Inc., Publishers
365 Broadway
Hillsdale, New Jersey 07642

Library of Congress Cataloging-in-Publication Data

Toward a unified theory of problem solving : views from the content
domains / edited by Mike U. Smith.
    p. cm.
  Includes bibliographical references.
  ISBN 0-8058-0510-9. -- ISBN 0-8058-0511-7 (pbk.)
  1. Problem solving. I. Smith, Mike U.
  B449.T68 1990
  153.4'3--dc20   90-33623
                                                   CIP

Printed in the United States of America

10 9 8 7 6 5 4 3 2 1

To those from whom I have learned—

my students and my teachers.

AUGUSTANA UNIVERSITY COLLEGE
LIBRARY ·

Contents

1
A VIEW FROM BIOLOGY   1
Mike U. Smith

2
A VIEW FROM CHEMISTRY   21
George M. Bodner

3
A VIEW FROM MEDICINE   35
Guy J. Groen and Villa L. Patel

4
A VIEW FROM PROGRAMMING   45
David N. Perkins, Steven Schwartz, and Rebecca Simmons

5
**A VIEW OF MATHEMATICAL PROBLEM SOLVING
   IN SCHOOL**   69
James G. Greeno

6
A VIEW FROM PHYSICS   99
Klaus Schultz and Jack Lochhead

7
A VIEW FROM TROUBLESHOOTING   115
Ray S. Perez

Preface

One of the most active fields of educational research in recent years has been the investigation of problem-solving performance. While the early studies were generally concerned with puzzles, chess, cryptarithmetic, and similar problems that are not "semantic rich," subsequent research has increasingly focused on problems within various content domains, especially mathematics and physics. Recent research in medicine and certain other domains has strongly emphasized the context specificity of the problem-solving process, suggesting that there are perhaps more differences than similarities among problem-solving performances in different domains. On the other hand, there is great similarity in many of the findings of these studies. These two opposing views of current problem-solving research lead to a variety of questions. Is problem solving a single construct? Are there aspects of problem-solving performance that are similar across a variety of content domains? What problem-solving skills learned within one context can be expected to transfer to other domains?

The story is told of three blind men who encountered an elephant in the jungle on a dark night. One felt of the trunk, one felt of a leg, and one felt of the tail. When asked what they had discovered, the first reported that an elephant must be like a great snake; the second said the elephant resembled the trunk of a great tree; and the third proposed that the beast was hard and thin like a whip. At least two issues explain the apparent confusion of these observers. First, their isolated observations do not appear to cohere, and second, there is specialization without communication among the specialists.

Until recently, research in problem solving was very similar to this state of affairs. Recent research in different content areas, however, has begun to reveal a host of commonalities. In April of 1988, a group of leading researcher educators was convened at the annual convention of the American Educational Research Association (AERA) in New Orleans to share research findings and to identify common results. Individuals representing the present state of knowledge of problem-solving research within each of several different domains of expertise participated. The symposium, which bore the same title as this book, drew considerable attention. Participants in this symposium were then invited to present their responses to the thoughts of the other presenters in New Orleans at the 1988 annual convention of the International Cognitive Science Society in Montreal. Based on these presentations, most of the participants developed position papers; these comprise the chapters of this book. One additional chapter (Perez) was

PREFACE

solicited to extend the range of domains considered to include troubleshooting. The result is a group of views about the consistencies within domain specific problem-solving research which should be useful to individuals involved in this research as well as to individuals interested in the current state of our theoretical understandings of problem solving within the content domains.

As I suggested in my opening remarks in the AERA symposium, attempting to construct a unified theory of problem solving is an awesome task, and the individual who proposes to do so is certainly presumptuous and perhaps foolhardy. Nevertheless, the similarities among recent findings within different domains is striking, and the time has clearly arrived to identify the commonalities and to attempt to construct them into some sort of consistent whole. The reader should take careful note, however, that the title of this volume was carefully chosen to indicate that our efforts are an attempt to bring us toward a unified theory of problem solving. We acknowledged from the outset that producing a unified theory was beyond our grasp at this time. Within areas other than problem solving, however, attempts to draw together such preliminary theoretical understandings have led to intense debate and disagreement, new questions and directions, and occasionally to new world views. It is the purpose of this book to serve as a basis for such productive exchange.

Several issues can be identified as common threads throughout many of the chapters that follow. A primary issue is definitional: What is a problem? The lack of consensus definitions of this (and other) terms in the literature is a source of some confusion and lack of generalizability among the conclusions of different studies. In Chapter 1, I propose a definition which is in keeping with most problem-solving research practice, although it is at variance with many of the currently published definitions.

The principle focus of most of the chapters is on the identification of common-alities within our research conclusions. Aspects of problem-solving performance at varying levels of expertise within each domain which appear to be equivalent to performances observed within other domains are identified. Several chapter authors review existing models of problem solving within their respective domains and/or attempt to develop models that would incorporate observations across domains.

A third recurrent issue is the transfer of problem-solving skills from one domain to another. If a skill is observed in the problem solving of individuals in disparate domains, to what extent should an individual who has learned this skill in one context be able to transfer that skill to another context readily? While this is not the same issue as the commonalities question above, the transfer question bears directly on any model of problem-solving performance and on the development of models of instruction in problem solving.

A final theme is closely related to the issue of transferability. Perkins et al. call it the "power-generality tradeoff." General problem-solving processes (e.g., working backward), which are widely applicable, have traditionally been called the "weak methods" because they are not as efficient and effective as the more domain specific, so-called "strong methods" typically used by domain experts. The more powerful a technique, the less generalizable it is to other domains. In contrast, there is a sense in which the more generalizable techniques are more powerful by virtue of the fact that they can be applied across a wider range of problems. This issue is important because it brings into focus the need for educators to consider carefully the balance in instruction between generalizable skills and domain-specific skills. It may be that we have too often focused on the "strong methods" which are of little value to our students outside of our classes.

In Chapter 1 I attempt to draw from the papers of the other authors and from research in general to develop a first approximation of what a unified theory of problem-solving might look like. Both internal and external factors that are thought to affect problem-solving performance are outlined. The propositions that result constitute a simplified model of problem solving which applies across content domains. This chapter also focuses on the difficult issue of defining the term "problem."

In Chapter 2 Bodner picks up the definitional issue, arriving at a conclusion opposite to that of Chapter 1 regarding the propriety of identifying exercises as problems. His arguments are well conceived and well presented. Clearly, neither position is "correct," but these two discussions do reveal a fundamental difference in the work of individuals who use these differing definitions. The performance of experts in a study of "exercise problem solving" would surely be different from the procedures that would be used by the same individuals in a study of solving "novel" problems. While no consensus definitions are likely to be achieved in the immediate future, it is clear that future studies should explicitly reveal their position on the problem/exercise issue. Bodner also reviews a number of the available stage models of problem solving before presenting a delightful, somewhat tongue-in-cheek, "anarchistic" model of problem solving.

Groen and Patel (Chapter 3) continue the theoretical analysis of problem solving based on their extensive studies of medical diagnosis. The result is a valuable theory of expertise, including models of novice and intermediate performance which are insightful.

PREFACE

Taking a broader approach to the entire issue, Perkins and his colleagues discuss the nature and roles of general vs. local knowledge in problem solving in Chapter 4. The dichotomy drawn relates directly to the domain specificity problem that was an initial focus of concern for the symposium participants. Late in the chapter, these authors address this problem in terms of the applicability of the procedures applied, noting the "power-generality tradeoff." Perkins also sheds additional light on the familiarity issue which is central to Bodner's arguments regarding the nature of exercises by focusing on different aspects of local knowledge to which an individual has either "pop-up" or "dig-out" access. Next, these authors discuss the transfer of problem-solving skills and present an extended example of how instruction can draw on these ideas so as to enhance the likelihood of transfer. Finally, these concepts are drawn into a "concept of mind" which is analogous to fractals.

Greeno (Chapter 5) reviews various models of solving math problems and their use in education. He makes an intriguing case that the most appropriate framework for understanding "math knowing" is as an "activity" instead of as a "set of cognitive structures and processes." Next Greeno provides an example of how this framework would inform the design of classroom instruction. The chapter also includes a general theoretical model of the nature of mathematical symbols and a consideration of current and future research problems in the area.

The book concludes with two chapters that focus more narrowly on research within two specific domains – physics and troubleshooting. Schultz and Lochhead (Chapter 6) identify four skills observed in physics problem solving which they propose as potentially transferable to other domains. In the final chapter Perez presents an informative analysis of research to date in troubleshooting. For those of us who are less familiar with trouble shooting malfunctions in diesel engines, bomber systems, etc. and with the training of individuals to perform these problem-solving tasks, this is an instructive chapter. Perez closes by bringing the reader full circle to the issue of the transferability of skills between different systems – an issue that is very important if we are to avoid the necessity of providing training for each individual piece of equipment and for every major modification of each instrument. The parallels between these training issues and instruction designed to teach students to become adept problem solvers in some general sense are readily apparent.

Have we accomplished our goal? Clearly a unified theory of problem solving has not been developed, but it is our hope that our syntheses have contributed to bringing the field closer to that goal. The value of this work must be judged by how well the propositions of our "theory" fit into a parsimonious whole, how well they describe the way in which people solve problems, and how useful our models are in research and in the classroom.

As with any task of this scope, many people have contributed in various ways to the outcome. I would like to thank all of the contributors, including Alan Schoenfeld who participated in the AERA symposium but was unable to contribute to this volume. We have also valued the thought-provoking comments of Richard Mayer and David Evans who served as discussants for the respective symposia. I would especially like to thank Vimla Patel who initially served as co-editor, as well as all of the individuals involved in the various typing, editing, and final production tasks.

1 A VIEW FROM BIOLOGY

Mike U. Smith
Mercer University

INTRODUCTION

This chapter is an attempt to critically analyze problem-solving research within the domain of biology, especially genetics, and to combine the conclusions of that analysis with a critical analysis of research in other disciplines so as to produce a unified theory of problem solving that would apply across content domains. This is truly a formidable task, and the result should be considered as only a first approximation of a statement of such a theory. The purpose of this work, therefore, is not to produce a definitive statement of a unified theory of problem solving, but to provide a target for discussion, criticism, and debate among problem-solving researchers and theorists. Such criticism is a routine and necessary part of the evolution of any theoretical construct.

Before any attempt is made to develop a statement of theory, one must first ask, what is a theory and how is the merit of a theory to be judged? According to Popper (1959), "Theories are [sets of] universal statements" (p. 27) or propositions. They serve two essential functions: explanation and prediction. Popper maintains that these statements delineate "universal concepts or names," (p. 74) that each statement must be a necessary part of the theory, that the statements taken collectively must be a sufficient summary of the theory, and that the theory must be free from contradiction. Turchin (1977) further suggests that a theory should be judged by 1) how well the statements describe reality, 2) the generality/predictive power of the statements, and 3) their "dynamic" nature, i.e., their ability to open new regions of study. The adequacy of the theory statement to be presented below should therefore be judged by whether or not it

1) proposes appropriate consensus definitions of critical terms,
2) adequately explains prior observations,
3) synthesizes observational data into a series of universal statements,
4) is parsimonious, and
5) leads to empirically testable predictions.

DEFINITION OF TERMS

One of the more troubling issues about which problem-solving researchers disagree is the exact meaning of some of the most basic terms that we use. Among these are such terms as "expert," "novice," "algorithm," "heuristic," "problem," and even "problem solving" itself, to name but a few. As any science student knows, the heart of any scientific discipline is a set of terms that have specific and widely accepted meanings, i.e., force, pressure, gene, acid, etc. Science courses that focus on acquiring these terms have, in fact, often been criticized as being equivalent to a course in a foreign language.

Why are terms, and specifically consensus definitions of terms, so important in the sciences? The basic answer to this question is simple: Shared meanings for terms allow accurate communication. When one physicist speaks to another about an "atom," there is no confusion about the meaning of the term. And if both these physicists report studies of nuclear magnetic resonance, you can be assured that they are referring to the same phenomenon.

It is not so in problem-solving research. The literature refers to social problems, alcohol and drug problems, students solving textbook problems, physicists solving "real" problems, etc. Any two problem-solving researchers may therefore be using the same word but with meanings that differ in substantive ways. Consider for example the following question: Do expert problem solvers usually use a forward-working or a backward-working (means-ends analysis) approach to problems? The answer to that question depends entirely upon your definition of the term "problem." Much of the literature reports that experts do indeed use a forward-working approach on typical textbook tasks that might be called "exercises" for these individuals. For non-routine tasks, however, experts often revert to an approach that more closely resembles the means-ends analysis approach of novices in the field.

Therefore, if the definition of "problem" includes exercises, the proper answer is that experts may use both approaches depending on the nature of the problem presented. If only non-routine, non-exercises are defined as problems, however, experts most often use a general means-ends analysis strategy. Therefore, if we are to be able to communicate with each other, we must make explicit our definitions of vague terms. And if we are to be able to compare the results of our research, we must achieve considerable agreement about what these definitions are. If we are to seek the commonalities in our findings, we must have common delimiters of the boundaries of the topic or at least an understanding of how our definitions vary. Without such definitions accurate communication is impossible.

The most important of the terms that are being used in our literature with varying interpretations is the term "problem" itself. There are almost as many definitions in print as there are researchers in the area, but no definition of the term has received wide acceptance. The following are some of the better known examples:

A problem is a "stimulus situation for which an organism does not have a response," . . . a problem arises "when the individual cannot immediately and effectively respond to the situation." (Woods, Crow, Hoffman, & Wright, 1985, p. 1)

"A person is confronted with a problem when he wants something and does not know immediately what series of actions he can perform to get it." (Newell & Simon, 1972, p. 72)

"Whenever there is a gap between where you are now and where you want to be, and you don't know how to find a way to cross that gap, you have a problem." (Hayes, 1980, p. i)

In their study of the arithmetic activity involved in everyday grocery shopping, Lave, Murtaugh, and de la Rocha (1984) propose that the shopper expects the task to proceed "unproblematically and effortlessly . . . It is in relation to this expectation that 'problems' take on meaning; they are viewed as *snags or interruptions*" (p. 79, emphasis added).

The definitions noted above appear to focus not on the nature of the task itself but upon the distance between the problem and the solver—the solver's lack of knowledge of an appropriate solution method. These "gap" definitions all sound quite similar. The principal difficulty with such definitions, however, is that in practice problem-solving research has not historically been so narrowly limited. Much of what is generally considered to be problem-solving research details the performance of subjects on classroom "problems" that are well structured and would typically be considered to be exercises. It is the solution of such exercises that is now well understood to include the application of domain-specific algorithms, the application of chunked procedural and conceptual knowledge, "pop-up" knowledge access, etc. If this narrow definition is accepted, then much of what we know about the performance of novices on such tasks and most of what we know about expertise is not accurately included in problem-solving theory. Most of the work to date (including my own) has compared the performance of novices and experts on the solution of problems that can only be considered to be "exercises" for the expert. Similarly, the extensive literature (see Davis, 1985) detailing our understanding of "routine" vs. "non-routine" problem solving would have to be eliminated since these definitions do not allow for "routine" problems.

The question is whether routine and non-routine problems are best considered to be apples and oranges or merely two varieties of the same fruit. Granted, there are fundamental differences in the performance of individuals on routine and non-routine tasks, but there are also fundamental similarities. Individuals completing both kinds of tasks use many of the same cognitive tools for both. They plan as necessary, break the problem into parts and attack parts separately, use domain-specific algorithms, attempt to bring their relevant domain knowledge to bear on the problem, use qualitative representations, check the accuracy of their work, etc. (see Smith, 1983). The question, therefore, is whether to focus on the similarities or the differences.

The issue here is a fundamental one: Is the status of a task as a problem an "innate characteristic of a task . . . [or a] subtle interaction between the task and the individual" (Bodner, this volume)? Put more simply, should "exercises" (tasks with which the solver is generally familiar and adept) be considered problems? Historically, the answer is clear: We have excluded exercises from our formal definitions but included them in our research. I would argue that we should use the more inclusive definition implied by our practice. Gap definitions are difficult to apply because they require a "floating" assessment. Tasks that are "problems" for one individual may not be for a different individual, and tasks that are problems for a person today may not be problems tomorrow. This may be an acceptable state of affairs, but it certainly makes the operational definition more difficult to apply.

A second set of issues revolves around the confusion that arises when terms (such as "problem") that are in common usage are also used by researchers. The multiple meanings of such terms in popular culture will necessarily cloud our understanding of the narrower scientific meanings of the terms. In genetics, for example, researchers have long recognized the student confusion that occurs from our technical usage of the term "dominant," a usage that is at variance with the common understanding of the term (e.g., dominant form of a gene vs. "dominant" person). Two common meanings of the term "problem" contribute to our confusion: 1) "difficult to deal with" and 2) "a source of perplexity or vexation" (Webster's Seventh New Collegiate Dictionary, 1971).

In the first sense, any task that is not difficult is not a problem. For example, "Making an A in his class is no problem." Or the one seen on student sweatshirts:

"I don't have a drinking problem. I drink. I get drunk. I fall down. No problem." Presumably routine tasks (exercises) would not be difficult and thus would not be considered problems to individuals familiar with these tasks. Also in this sense, only tasks that are sufficiently complex would be considered to be "real" problems.

In the second sense of everyday usage, if my wife and I are having marital difficulties, that is a "problem". The student with the sweatshirt may not think he has a drinking problem, but his/her parents may view the situation as "problematic." The central characteristic of this kind of "problem" is the perplexity encountered by the solver—the person doesn't immediately know what to do. For purposes of our research, however, I maintain that perplexity is not a necessary component of problem solving. The principal reason for this position is the fact that problem solvers often exhibit many common behaviors whether they find the task perplexing or not. If the challenge is so perplexing as to be overwhelming, in fact, this aspect of the problem may paralyze the system so that effective problem-solving techniques cannot be appropriately summoned and applied.

Problems that are perplexing, for which we have no "immediate and effective" response, do indeed call forth additional and sometimes altogether different problem-solving behaviors. On the other hand, I also find various genetics exercises to be challenging "problems" even though I have a ready store of strategies, heuristics, and algorithms with which I can "immediately and effectively" respond. That such exercises do not perplex me seems an artificial and extraneous constraint on the definition.

A third issue related to common usage of the term "problem" that has crept into the literature is the fact that the word is often equated with the term "question." Not all questions, however, should be considered to be problems. For example, is "What does 2 + 2 equal?" a problem? Or, "What phenotypic ratios are expected among the offspring of a monohybrid cross between two heterozygotes?" This latter type of item has occasionally been included in studies of genetics "problem solving" and is often included on typical genetics exams in a section of "problems," but I would argue that such items should not be defined as problems. How do such questions differ from any other memorization item? Would you consider "What is the capital of the United States?" to be a problem? Probably not.

Perhaps again the common usage of the term causes the confusion. If a student is faced with the question on a test but doesn't know that the expected ratio is three to one or that the U.S. capital is Washington, DC, then he does indeed have a "problem"/difficulty. The vast majority of the mental tools that can be applied to problems that cannot be solved by memorization, however, cannot be applied to ameliorate this difficulty. This is not a "problem" in what must be called the "technical" meaning of the term (vs. "common usage"). The solution of a problem must require more than simple recognition or recall from memory.

Similarly, problems cannot be solved algorithmically, i.e., with little or no understanding of what has been done or why it was correct. Landa (1972) defines an algorithm as a "completely determined . . . ready-made prescription on how to act" (p. 21, 23, 24). Lochhead and Collura (1981) add that algorithms can be "black boxes used to produce answers" (p. 47) with little or no understanding. By analogy, is reproducing a diagram that may have appeared in the text or on the blackboard during class solving a problem? Is identically repeating a series of steps solving a problem? I maintain that it is not. Developing the ability to reproduce a pattern and do it appropriately may indeed be <u>learning</u>, but performing the task is not problem solving.

Algorithms are a basic part of the procedural repertoire of any skilled problem solver. This issue of concern here is whether or not the algorithm is applied mindlessly ("algorithmically") or with understanding. My earlier position (cited by Bodner in this volume) was that tasks that could be solved by a single algorithm should not be considered to be problems. The selection of appropriate algorithms and their modification to accommodate the unique aspects of a problem, however, are often important aspects of problem solving. The mindless application of algorithms, often to situations in which they are inappropriate, is in fact a recognized distinction between successful and unsuccessful problem solvers (Smith, 1983). The distinction at issue here is whether or not the task requires analysis and reason that must be based on an understanding of the content involved.

On the other hand, tasks that can be solved by the application of an algorithm cannot be considered problems in situations that do not require selecting the algorithm and evaluating how it may or may not need to be modified in the present task. This circumstance is all too familiar to many students who learn to carry out a given algorithm and are then presented with tasks to which that algorithm is appropriately applicable. Responding to such stimulus tasks requires no analysis or reasoning but is instead reminiscent of Pavlovian conditioning.

Perhaps the decision of whether or not to include exercises as problems should be affected most by the goals of the research that seeks to understand problem solving. Much of this research is designed to understand problem solving in the classroom and, thereby, to impact the classroom instruction of problem solving. Clearly, much of classroom problem solving involves tasks that would be considered exercises. There may initially be a "gap" between the task and the student, i.e., he or she may not know how to achieve a solution, but the teacher does not typically terminate the lesson after the student has solved a single problem of a type. Much of what the classroom teacher is interested in is solving tasks that are exercises for both him or her and for many of the students—tasks for which the student knows appropriate solution procedures but has yet to become adept at applying these procedures or at matching these procedures to appropriate problems. If these exercises are not to be considered problem solving, then a large proportion of the research in problem solving will have little to say to the classroom teacher.

The crux of the exercise/problem issue may in fact reflect nothing more than our differing goals in the classroom. As a genetics teacher, I want to help my students become good problem solvers, but my primary goal in assigning students genetics problems is to help them to achieve a greater depth of understanding about the content. Students can often parrot back verbatim definitions of such terms as "gene," "allele," and "segregation" and even label diagrams of cell division, but the student who can apply that knowledge to the solution of a genetics problem has clearly achieved a deeper level of understanding of those terms and processes. In fact, I often tell students that getting the right answer is not nearly as important as understanding what's going on in the problem.

In practice, teachers who are involved in training medical doctors or other professionals do not have that luxury. The goal is to develop individuals who can indeed solve the ill-defined, non-routine, perplexing, complex, real-world problems that they will encounter on the job. While there is a place for learning to solve routine problems early in the training of professionals, such education cannot focus solely on problems that would be considered to be exercises. Would-be professionals must develop the ability to address a task "when they don't know what to do" since uncertainty is certainly a hallmark of problem-solving in the real-world context. My guess is that this fact underlies our different positions on the exercise/problem issue.

A Continuum Definition

To summarize the above, differences among definitions of the term "problem" focus on two principal issues: a) differences between the ways in which the term has historically been formally defined and used in practice and b) whether or not the status of a task is an innate characteristic of the task or is dependent upon the distance between the task and the problem-solving abilities of the solver. This distance is described in terms of familiarity with the problem or problem type, uncertainty as to how to proceed, perplexity, difficulty, and complexity. A principal difficulty with "gap" definitions, however, is that it is impossible to determine when an individual is (sufficiently) familiar with a task that it should no longer be considered a "problem," or just how complex or perplexing a task must be in order to be considered a "problem". The terms used to describe the "gap" are clearly descriptors for continua, not for discrete dichotomies (see Figure 1). What I am proposing, therefore, is a "continuum definition," a definition that (within the limits detailed above) embraces all tasks that fall along the continua from exercise to "real problem," from simple to complex, from familiar to unfamiliar:

easy ———————————————————— **hard**

simple ————————————————— **complex**

familiar ————————————————— **unfamiliar**

straight-forward ——————————— **perplexity**

exercise ————————————— **"real" problem**

Figure 1.   Problem continua.

A problem is any task that requires analysis and reasoning toward a goal (or "solution"). This analysis and reasoning must be based on an understanding of the domain from which the task is drawn. A problem cannot be solved by recall, recognition, or reproduction (see Figure 2). Whether or not a task is defined as a problem is not determined by how difficult or by how perplexing it is for the intended solver. "Problem solving," therefore, becomes the process by which a system generates an acceptable solution to such a problem.

This definition is proffered, not to add to the plethora of definitions already available, but in the hope that it will encourage researchers to note the ambiguities in our historical use of the term. I also hope that this definition will serve as a focus for lively discussion among researchers which will bring us closer to consensus definitions and clear communication. Realistically, of course, I recognize that it is unlikely that any definitions will be widely accepted in the near future. Nevertheless, the delineation of the definitional issue above is intended to encourage researchers to identify their personal positions on these definitional issues, to acknowledge those positions, to consider how the definitions they apply impact their research, and to be alert to ways in which definitional differences among researchers limit the comparability of their findings.

FACTORS AFFECTING PROBLEM-SOLVING PERFORMANCE

Using these definitions, we can now seek those aspects of problem solving that are common across a variety of domains.

External Factors

Research in several domains demonstrates that the performance of the problem solver is narrowly delimited by the nature of the problem being solved. Among those characteristics critical to determining how a problem will be solved are the domain from which the problem is drawn, the form in which the problem is presented (including the language used), and the complexity of the problem (Cassels & Johnstone, 1984; Gabel & Sherwood, 1984; Simon & Hayes, 1976). Individuals are more successful at solving problems within their domain of expertise than in other domains (see Patel, Arocha, & Groen, 1986.) Problem-solving success is also affected by the surrounding social environment of the problem solver, e.g., peer pressure, peer cooperation, teacher and parental expectations, etc. (see Rogoff & Gardner, 1984). These factors may have either a positive or a negative effect on the process.

Internal Factors

A considerable body of literature (see Bodner, Carter, & Bowen, 1988; Paris,

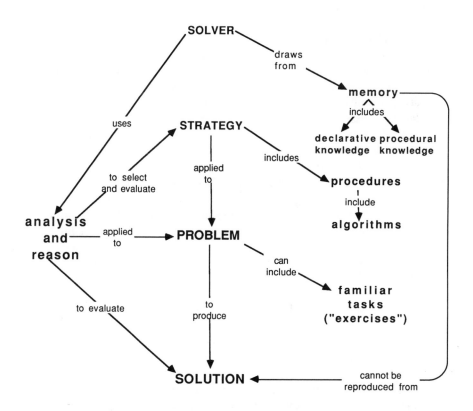

Figure 2. A pictorial definition of the term "problem."

1988; Schoenfeld, 1988) demonstrates that good problem solving is enhanced by certain affective variables, including self-confidence, perseverance, enjoyment, positive self talk, motivation, beliefs, and values. The extensive expert-novice literature also demonstrates that the length of prior successful problem-solving experience of the individual — both at solving problems in general and at solving problems in this domain in particular — is also a determinant of both the procedures that will be applied and the degree of problem-solving success (see Smith & Good, 1984.)

Good problem solving is enhanced by knowledge of general problem-solving procedures. Good problem solvers know what, how, and when to apply these techniques. These include means-ends analysis/backward reasoning, forward reasoning, reasoning by analogy, hypothesis generation and testing, trial and error, estimation, etc. (see Lochhead, 1988; Smith & Good, 1984).

The performance of the solver is determined by the relevant knowledge that he has and its accessibility. First an adequate, well-organized, and easily accessible conceptual/schematic knowledge of the relevant content domain is required (Chi, Feltovich, & Glaser, 1981; Moll & Allen, 1982; Perkins, Schwartz, & Simmons, 1988; Smith & Good, 1984). This knowledge serves as the basis upon which the solver analyzes the problem, reasons toward a solution, and assesses the appropriateness of the solution. For the successful problem solver, this knowledge is free of various domain-specific misconceptions or erroneous beliefs that impede the solutions of less successful solvers (Smith & Good, 1984). In addition to a conceptual understanding, problem solving requires procedural knowledge, both general and domain-specific. This includes not only a knowledge of the different strategies, heuristics, algorithms, shortcuts, etc. that are relevant, but also the constraints under which each can be applied. Essentially, procedural knowledge consists of knowing what to do, when to do it, and how to do it (Smith, 1983). The solver's conceptual/schematic knowledge of the content involved in the problem further provides the solver with an understanding of why various procedures are appropriate, allowing him to modify his performance as necessary for each unique problem.

Finally, problem solving is enhanced by chunking the solver's knowledge; that is, the individual bits of the solver's knowledge (conceptual, procedural, and experiential) are organized into larger groups or "chunks" much as a chess expert recognizes and recalls groups of chess piece positions as opposed to the positions of individual pieces (deGroot, 1965; Simon, 1981). Such chunking not only decreases the demands placed on the solver's working memory, but also allows for the triggering of appropriate procedures, bits of conceptual knowledge, and memories of related experiences at one time (Chi et al., 1981). Such coordination likely contributes to problem-solving success.

The performance of the problem solver is also delimited by the personal characteristics of the solver. The individual brings a range of general aptitudes or capabilities to the task. The level of (Piagetian) cognitive development (Walker, Hendrix, & Mertens, 1980; Smith, 1983) and field independence (Witkin, Oltman, Raskin, & Karp, 1971) are two such general competencies that have been shown to correlate with the ability to solve problems in various domains . In particular, the ability of the formal operational individual to "think about his or her own thinking," to review and analyze the process of problem solving, contributes to the ability to identify, modify, and adopt successful problem-solving patterns. Similarly, field independent individuals are presumably more able to abstract the relevant information in the problem from the irrelevant "background noise" (Falls & Voss, 1985).

A MODEL OF SUCCESSFUL PROBLEM SOLVING

First, I would argue from a research perspective that expert problem solving is not identical to successful problem solving. Most experts are indeed successful problem solvers, but our research has continually identified exceptional novice subjects whose problem-solving techniques are very similar to those of experts. Such novices can successfully solve problems given an adequate introduction to and practice in the domain (see Smith & Good, 1984). Studying the performance of domain experts has been a fruitful research tool as for identifying successful problem solvers. Analysis of the performance of "successful novices," however, reveals certain differences between their problem solving and that of experts in the domain. In particular, these subjects are typically more informative since much less of what they know and do is tacit information than it is in the expert subject. In addition, their performance is not confounded by the extraneous variable of experience. In most academic settings (with medical diagnosis and electronic troubleshooting as notable exceptions) the educational goal is to produce successful problem solvers and not "experts" as such. I suggest, therefore, that our focus should turn to understanding the performance of successful solvers at a variety of levels. From this vantage point, expert problem solving is a subset of successful problem solving. It is certainly a valuable area of study, especially in fields such as medicine, but it is not the entire story.

What is it then that good problem solvers do that contributes to their success and distinguishes their performance from that of unsuccessful subjects? And what are the commonalities to be found in this performance, not only in biology, but also across disciplines?

First, the problem solver creates an internal "problem space," i.e., a personal understanding of the problem (Newell & Simon, 1972); (see Figure 1). Considerable research has shown that for the successful problem solver this phase of the solution process involves the representation of the problem in terms that the solver understands, that focus on the relationship of the given problem to the solver's knowledge (including similarities to previously solved problems), and that extract the most important components of the problem in such a way as to contribute to the ease of selection and implementation of subsequent steps (i.e., decreasing the demands on working memory; Hinsley, Hayes, & Simon, 1977; Pople, 1977; Wortman, 1972). The recognition of problem similarities, i.e., that the given problem is an instantiation of a more general problem category or type, is particularly valuable since this recognition provides for the triggering of related chunks of content and procedural and experiential knowledge that will guide the subsequent solution process (Chi et al., 1981). This representation is often a qualitative one even when the task requires a quantitative solution (Larkin, Heller, & Greeno, 1980; Lochhead, 1988).

Certain aspects of this phase have also been called redescription since the solver often abstracts salient problem features and describes them in a different manner. The most well-known example of this process is the use of free body diagrams and vectors in physics (Larkin, 1980a). In algebra word problems the redescription of the problem as an equality (formula) often constitutes the most significant part of the solution to the problem. Recent work with problems that approximate real world genetics laboratory data have also supported this observation (Streibel, Stewart, Koedinger, Collins, & Jungck, 1987). The development of a conducive initial problem space clearly depends upon the use of an adequate knowledge base.

Early on the successful problem solver may also plan the basic outlines of the general strategy or approach to be taken in the solution process. The following brief excerpts from the verbal protocols of two subjects as they solve genetics problems demonstrate such planning:

> Subject E04 reads the problem aloud, then stares silently at the problem statement.
> I: Can you tell me what you're doing?
> E04:   I'm trying to figure out how to set it up. You have to set up all the possible combinations of four children that you could get. And then you need to calculate the percentage — the probability — that you get each one, and get the probability for each group. And then you have to see how many of those, then, at the end, end up having two sons.
> N09:   I'll figure out what the offspring will be and then I'll figure out the ratios. (Smith, 1983, p. 202)

Such planning may or may not occur depending on the perceived complexity of the problem. Planning may also be tacit (not in conscious awareness) for more experienced solvers.

Next, the successful solver applies relevant problem-solving procedures to the task. The solver draws from an arsenal of two types of heuristics. The first are often called the general or weak heuristics because they are broadly applicable across a variety of domains but are typically inefficient in ensuring the rapid achievement of an appropriate solution. On the other hand, such heuristics should perhaps be considered as robust since they can be used effectively (if not efficiently) in many different areas. It is these heuristics that successful problem solvers typically apply to problems in areas in which they are not expert and that are most often the focus of present problem-solving courses. For example, all successful problem solvers tend to break a complex problem into its component parts which are then addressed individually. Other prominent examples of these techniques include trial-and-error and means-ends analysis.

Within areas in which an individual has more experience, the typical solver is more likely to use what Larkin (1980b) calls a "knowledge development" or forward chaining approach. Instead of working backwards (means-ends analysis), such individuals tend to "work forward" from the given conditions in the problem statement, applying appropriate procedures to derive new information from them until the desired information is reached. The understanding that knowledge about the problem is being developed during the solution process is a hallmark of successful problem solving. In this way the solver modifies his or her internal problem space as more is learned about the problem. The solver must therefore also maintain a knowledge of his or her current position along the solution path. Two brief genetics problem protocol examples are instructive.

E02:   I do not remember, by the way, which chromosomes those things were on, or whether they were sex-linked or linked at all. So, ah, let's see. . . . Well, it should be buried in here somewhere.
I: What do you mean?
E02:   Ah, we'll know what the linkage is when the problem is solved. Let's see.

E05:   I'm just gonna work through some other problems and get some other, other information about the genotype. (Smith, 1983)

The second type of heuristic available to the solver is domain-specific heuristics and algorithms. These techniques are generally applicable only to problems within a defined domain such as genetics and tend to be a focus of courses within these disciplines. Examples in genetics include writing down an explicit definition key for the allele symbols used, drawing all possible separate gametes, and drawing a Punnett square. These tools are very powerful in achieving quick and accurate problem solutions, but their implementation requires an adequate understanding of the content domain, of the events represented, of the criteria that must be met in order for them to be properly applied, and of how the techniques must be modified to accommodate various nuances in problems. Applying these procedures, analyzing when they are appropriate, modifying them as appropriate in the present problem, combining the results of different problem parts, and interpreting the results into a problem solution requires logical analysis and reason (Smith & Good, 1984).

Competent problem solvers are also able to perform multi-step procedures when necessary, keeping the results of previous steps in mind (Smith, 1983). In contrast, unsuccessful problem solvers are particularly prone to attempt only one-step solution procedures whether appropriate or not. For example, in an earlier study (Smith, 1983), after reading the problem statement, asking several questions, and making some irrelevant observations about the pedigree presented, Subject N03 said, "I would say something like four to one. It's just a guess. I don't think there's not, there's much probability for red head [among the offspring]" (p. 148).

Even when attempting procedures that are indeed more complex, these individuals often appear to be unable to maintain an adequate knowledge of what they have done before and to question how previous work might relate to the present position in the problem solution. Their attentional focus appears to be markedly too narrow to facilitate a correct solution, perhaps related to their lack of chunking of knowledge about the domain and even about the problem solution to this point.

After a solution is generated, most unsuccessful subjects stop immediately. For most successful subjects, on the other hand, the final phase of the solution process is the subsequent evaluation of the solution. Again, this procedure has been noted by researchers in a variety of domains where it has been termed "solution assessment" (Reif, 1980), verification (Schoenfeld & Herrman, 1980; Wallas, 1926), looking back (Polya, 1957), and checking (Smith & Good, 1984). This process can take many forms depending on the problem. It may involve a qualitative review as to the reasonability of the solution achieved, a check of the accuracy of the solver's work (mathematics, logic, etc.), and/or an assessment of the similarity of the solution to solutions achieved previously in related problems.

SUMMARY OF PROPOSITIONS

A. Definitions

A problem is a task that requires analysis and reasoning toward a goal (the "solution"); must be based on an understanding of the domain from which the task is drawn; cannot be solved by recall, recognition, reproduction, or application of an algorithm alone; and is not determined by how difficult or by how perplexing the task is for the intended solver.

B. External factors affecting problem-solving performance

1. Problem Context. Successful problem solving is more likely in problems couched within a familiar/well-understood context.

2. Problem Structure. Problem-solving success is affected by the structure of the problem itself, i.e., semantics, vocabulary, novelty, complexity, etc.

3. Social factors. Problem-solving success is affected by the surrounding social environment of the problem solver, e.g., peer pressure, peer cooperation, teacher and parental expectations, etc.

C. Internal factors affecting problem-solving performance

1. Affect. Good problem solving is enhanced by certain affective variables, including self-confidence, perseverance, enjoyment, positive self-talk, motivation, beliefs, and values.

2. Experience. Good problem solving is enhanced by the length of prior successful problem-solving experience (especially in the domain of the problem).

3. Domain-Specific Knowledge. Good problem solving requires knowledge of the domain from which the problem is drawn. This knowledge is of three types: factual, conceptual or schematic, and procedural.

4. General Problem-Solving Knowledge. Good problem solving is enhanced by knowledge of general problem-solving procedures such as means-ends analysis, trial-and-error, etc.

5. The problem solver's knowledge must be:
adequate, organized/accessible/integrated, and accurate (misconception free).

6. Other personal characteristics. Problem-solving success is also affected by the solver's level of cognitive development, relative field dependence, personality, etc.

D. Characteristics of good problem solving:

Good problem solvers tend to

1. adapt their knowledge and its organization to facilitate the solution of problems in a domain (Lochhead, 1988);

2. apply their knowledge and skills to the problem-solving task;

3. use forward reasoning and domain-specific procedures on standard problems within their domain of expertise, but use the "weaker"

problem-solving procedures (means-ends analysis, trial-and-error, etc.) on problems outside their domain of expertise;

4. create an internal "problem space" which incorporates a qualitative representation or redescription of the problem;

5. plan (at least tacitly) the general strategy or approach to be taken (depending on the perceived complexity of the problem);

6. break problems into parts and perform multi-step procedures when necessary, keeping the results of previous steps in mind;

7. employ relevant problem-solving procedures/heuristics—both do-main-specific and general;

8. evaluate the solution and the solution procedure; and

9. abstract patterns in their own performance (identify powerful solution strategies) and identify critical similarities among problems (identify useful problem types).

Expert (highly experienced), as compared to novice, problem solvers tend to

1. be more successful at solving problems;

2. solve problems more rapidly;

3. apply procedures more tacitly ("automatically");

4. organize and apply their knowledge (including knowledge of procedures) in "chunks"; and

5) be able to recall more of the critical features of the problem-solving task.

SUGGESTED DIRECTIONS FOR FUTURE RESEARCH

The most obvious next step required is a careful analysis by and ongoing dialogue among researchers in response to the propositions I have proposed. How well do they meet the criteria outlined earlier?

The second direction for research that is clearly implied by these propositions is a more careful attention to the distinctions between expertise and success. Since no one can become an expert in all the domains in which he needs to adequately solve problems, what are the characteristics of good problem solvers who are not highly experienced professionals (experts)? A correlate of this issue is the nature of expertise. A recent study that compared genetic counselors and genetics faculty (Smith, 1988) suggests that some of our understanding of expertise is perhaps applicable only to educators in the domain of interest. Similar studies of other non-educator experts should be conducted.

A third direction for future research is a greater emphasis on the issues of the development and teaching of problem-solving skills. The absence of propositions relating to these issues from the statements above is conspicuous.

ACKNOWLEDGMENT

This chapter is based in part on work supported by the National Science Foundation under Grant No. MDR 8609356.

REFERENCES

Bodner, G. M., Carter, C. S., & Bowen, C. (1988, April). *Toward a unified theory of problem solving: A view from chemistry.* Paper presented at the meeting of the American Educational Research Association, New Orleans, LA.

Cassels, J.R.T., & Johnstone, A.H. (1984). The effect of language on student performance on multiple choice tests in chemistry. *Journal of Chemical Education, 61,* 613-615.

Chi, M.T.H., Feltovitch, P.J., & Glaser, R. (1981). Categorization and representation of physics problems by experts and novices. *Cognitive Science, 5,* 121-152.

Davis, R. B. (1985). Solving the "three switch" problem: A case study. *Journal of Mathematical Behavior, 4,* 281-291.

deGroot, A.D., (1965). *Thought and choice in chess.* The Hague: Mouton.

Falls, T.H., & Voss, B. (1985, April). *The ability of high school chemistry students to solve computational problems requiring proportional reasoning as affected by item in-task variables.* Paper presented at the meeting of the National Association for Research in Science Teaching, French Lick Springs, IN.

Gabel, D.L., & Sherwood, R.D. (1984). Analyzing difficulties with mole-concept tasks by using familiar analog tasks. *Journal of Research in Science Teaching, 21,* 843-851.

Hayes, J. (1980). *The complete problem solver.* Philadelphia: The Franklin Institute Press.

Hinsley, D.A., Hayes, J.R., & Simon, H.A. (1977). From words to equations: Meaning and representation in algebra word problems. In M.A. Just & P.A. Carpenter (Eds.), *Cognitive processes in comprehension* (pp. 89 - 106). Hillsdale, NJ: Lawrence Erlbaum Associates.

Landa, L. N. (1972). *Algorithmization in learning and instruction.* Englewood Cliffs, NJ: Educational Technology Publications.

Larkin, J.H. (1980a). *Spatial reasoning in solving physics problems* (C.I.P. #434). Unpublished manuscript, Carnegie-Mellon University, Pittsburgh, PA.

Larkin, J.H. (1980b). Teaching problem solving in physics: The psychological laboratory and the practical classroom. In D.T. Tuma & F. Reif (Eds.), *Problem solving and education: Issues in teaching and research.* Hillsdale, NJ: Lawrence Erlbaum Associates.

Larkin, J.H., Heller, J.I., & Greeno, J.G. (1980). Instructional implications of research on problem solving. *New Directions for Teaching and Learning, 2,* 51-65.

Lave, J., Murtaugh, M., & de la Rocha, P. (1984). The dialectic of arithmetic in grocery shopping. In B. Rogoff & J. Lave (Eds.), *Everyday cognition: Its development in social context* (pp. 67-94). Cambridge, MA: Harvard University Press.

Lochhead, J. (1988, April). *Toward a unified theory of problem solving: A view from physics.* Paper presented at the meeting of the American Educational Research Association, New Orleans, LA.

Lochhead, J., & Collura, J. (1981). A cure for the cookbook laboratories. *The Physics Teacher, 19,* 46 - 50.

Moll, M.B., & Allen, R.D. (1982). Developing critical thinking skills in biology. *Journal of College Science Teaching, 12,* 95 - 98.

Newell, A., & Simon, H.A. (1972) *Human problem solving.* Englewood Cliffs, NJ: Prentice Hall.

Patel, V.L., Arocha, J.F., & Groen, G.J. (1986). Strategy selection and degree of expertise in clinical reasoning. *Proceedings of the Annual Conference of the Cognitive Science Society,* 780-791.

Perkins, D.N., Schwartz, S. & Simmons, R. (1988, April). *Toward a unified theory of problem solving; A view from programming.* Paper presented at the meeting of the American Educational Research Association, New Orleans, LA.

Polya, G. (1957) *How to solve it.* Garden City, NY: Doubleday.

Pople, H.E. (1977, August). The formation of composite hypotheses in diagnostic problem solving: An exercise in synthetic reasoning. *Proceedings of the 5th International Joint Conference on Artificial Intelligence.* Cambridge, MA.

Popper, K.R. (1959). *The logic of scientific discovery.* New York: Basic.

Reif, F. (1980). Theoretical and educational concerns with problem solving: Bridging the gaps with human cognitive engineering. In D.T. Tuma & R. Reif (Eds.), *Problem-solving and education: Issues in teaching and research* (pp. 39-50). Hillsdale, NJ: Lawrence Erlbaum Associates.

Rogoff, B., & Gardner, W. (1984). Adult guidance of cognitive development. In B. Rogoff & J. Lave (Eds.), *Everyday cognition: Its development in social context* (pp. 95-116). Cambridge, MA: Harvard University Press.

Schoenfeld, A.H. (1988, April). *A view from mathematical cognition.* Paper presented at the meeting of the American Educational Research Association, New Orleans, LA.

Schoenfeld, A.H., & Herrmann, D.J. (1980). *Problem perception and knowledge structure in expert and novice mathematics problem solvers.* Clinton, NY: National Science Foundation. (ERIC Document Reproduction Service No. ED 200 609)

Simon, H.A. (1981). Information-processing models of cognition. *Journal of the American Society for Information Science, 32,* 364-377.

Simon, H.A., & Hayes, J.R. (1976). The understanding process; Problem isomorphs. *Cognitive Psychology, 8,* 165-190.

Smith, M. U. (1983). A comparative analysis of the performance of experts and novices while solving selected classical genetics problems (Doctoral dissertation, The Florida State University, 1983). *Dissertation Abstracts International, 44,* 451A.

Smith, M.U. (1988). *Expertise, knowledge structures, and expertise in classical genetics.* Manuscript submitted for publication.

Smith, M.U., & Good, R. (1984). Problem solving and classical genetics: Successful versus unsuccessful performance. *Journal of Research in Science Teaching, 21,* 895-912.

Striebel, M.J., Stewart, J., Koedinger, K., Collins, A., & Jungck, J.R. (1987). Mendel: An intelligent computer tutoring system for genetics problem-solving, conjecturing, and understanding. *Machine Mediated Learning, 2,* 129-159.

Turchin, V. F. (1977). *The phenomenon of science* (B. Frentz, Trans.). New York: Columbia University Press.

Walker, R.A., Hendrix, J.R., & Mertens, T.R. (1980). Sequenced instruction in genetics and Piagetian cognitive development. *American Biology Teacher, 42,* 104-108.

Wallas, G. (1926). *The art of thought.* New York: Carcourt.

Webster's seventh new collegiate dictionary. (1971). Springfield, MA: Merriam Company.

Witkin, H.A., Oltman, P.K., Raskin, E., & Karp, S.A. (1971). *A manual for the embedded figures tests.* Palo Alto, CA: Consulting Psychologists Press.

Woods, D. R., Crowe, C. M., Hoffman , T. W., & Wright, J. D. (1985, January). Challenges to teaching problem solving skills. *Chem 13 News,* No. 155, pp. 1-12. Waterloo, Ontario, Canada: University of Waterloo.

Wortman, P.M. (1972). Medical diagnosis: An information processing approach. *Computers and Biomedical Research, 5,* 315-328.

2 A VIEW FROM CHEMISTRY

George M. Bodner
Purdue University

INTRODUCTION

For months, I have been agonizing over the question posed by the organizers of this symposium: "Is it possible to produce a unified theory of problem solving?" I have waffled back and forth between an optimistic "yes" and a pessimistic "no." While sitting in a hotel room, just before leaving for the tenth annual conference of the Cognitive Science Society, I came to the following conclusion: Yes, it is possible to construct a unified theory of problem solving. I have done so, and I expect that each of the other participants in this symposium will have done so as well. Unfortunately, I'm afraid our unified theories will differ significantly from one another. I am confident that we are beyond the stage described by Figure 1, but I fear that there are subtle differences between the way each of us defines important terms, which cause difficulties in reaching a truly unified theory of problem solving. Researchers in this area, as much as any I've encountered, seem to adhere to a philosophy summarized by Lewis Carroll (1896).

"When I use a word," Humpty Dumpty said in a rather scornful tone, it means just what I choose it to mean — neither more nor less. (p. 119)

We can't even agree among ourselves about the meaning of the word "problem," much less "problem solving." In his AERA paper, Mike Smith (1988) reported that he had disagreed with Don Woods about whether successful problem solvers most often used a forward-working versus means-ends analysis approach to problem solving. He then noted that the confusion was resolved when he realized that Woods does not consider the solution of exercises to be problem solving.

Smith (1988) argues cogently for including solving exercises as a subset of problem solving. To ensure debate, I'm going to disagree. I'm also going to question the notion that the difference between exercises and problems is one of "difficulty" or "complexity." Finally, I am going to question the assertion that individuals solving exercises use many of the same strategies they apply to problems. I don't question the validity of studying the solving of exercises, I just don't believe this is relevant to discussions of problem solving.

DEFINITIONS OF TERMS

Unlike many others, I do not feel compelled to introduce new definitions of terms. Let me simply state the operational set of definitions I will use in this chapter. Hayes (1980) defined a problem as follows:

Whenever there is a gap between where you are now and where you want to be, and you don't know how to find a way to cross that gap, you have a problem. (p. i.)

More recently, Wheatley (1984) coined the consummate definition of problem solving:

What you do, when you don't know what to do. (p. 1.)

Let me conclude this section by introducing a working definition of the term *algorithm* (Ehrlich, Flexner, Carruth, & Hawkins, 1980).

Rules for calculating something that can be followed more or less automatically by a reasonably intelligent system, such as a computer. (p. 17.)

LOGICAL CONSEQUENCES OF THESE DEFINITIONS

If you accept these definitions, there is a fundamental difference between an exercise and a problem. We all routinely encounter questions or tasks for which we don't know the answer, but we feel confident that we know how to obtain the answer. When this happens, when we know the sequence of steps needed to cross the gap between where we are and where we want to be, we are faced with an exercise not a problem.

Smith (1988) eliminates from classification as a problem any task that can be solved completely by an algorithm. I agree. By listening in class, by reading examples in the text, and, most importantly, by working similar questions on their own, most of my students construct an algorithm that turns the following question into an exercise.

What is the empirical formula of a compound of xenon and oxygen that is 67.2% Xe and 32.8% O? (Carter, LaRussa, & Bodner, 1987, p. 653).

In fact, I would argue — in accord with Johnstone and El-Banna (1986) — that it is the existence of a well-defined algorithm, constructed from their prior experience (Bodner, 1986), that turns this question into an exercise for so many of my students.

There is no innate characteristic of a task that inevitably makes it a problem. Status as a problem is a subtle interaction between the task and the individual struggling to find an appropriate answer or solution (Bodner, 1987). The following question, for example, is a problem for most students when they begin their study of chemistry:

Magnesium reacts with oxygen to form magnesium oxide.

$$2\ Mg(s) + O_2(g) \longrightarrow 2\ MgO(s)$$

What weight of oxygen is required to burn 10.0 grams of magnesium?

To their instructors, however, it is an exercise. They have done so many similar calculations that they almost instantly recognize that they can convert grams of magnesium into moles of magnesium, moles of magnesium into moles of oxygen, and then moles of oxygen into grams of oxygen. Similarly, while the task in Figure 2 would be a problem for most readers of this chapter, it is no more than a routine exercise for chemists who specialize in organic synthesis.

The difference between an exercise and a problem is not a question of difficulty, or complexity, but one of familiarity. Patel and Groen noted that expert physicians explained routine medical diagnosis problems by a process of forward reasoning. They also noted that "forward reasoning is associated with successful performance and tends to disappear when a subject is uncertain or unsuccessful" (p. 8). I am not surprised. I would argue that the more likely that the protocol from a "problem-solving" interview can be analyzed as an example of forward-chaining or forward-working, the more likely the individual will be successful because he or she was working an exercise — a task with which he or she is familiar.

THE ROLE OF ALGORITHMS IN WORKING
EXERCISES AND PROBLEMS

Consider the algorithm used to solve the following question:

What is the empirical formula of a compound of xenon and oxygen that is 67.2% Xe and 32.8% O?

Our students are taught to assume that they start with a 100-gram sample of the compound, which therefore contains 67.2 grams of xenon and 32.8 grams of oxygen. They are then taught to convert grams of each element into moles of the element.

67.2 g Xe x $\frac{1 \text{ mol Xe}}{131.30 \text{ g}}$ = 0.512 mol Xe

32.8 g O x $\frac{1 \text{ mol O}}{15.9994 \text{ g}}$ = 2.05 mol O

Finally, they are taught to divide the number of moles of xenon into the number of moles of oxygen to find the ratio of these elements

$\frac{2.05 \text{ mol O}}{0.512 \text{ mol Xe}}$ = 4.00

and thereby conclude that the empirical formula of the compound is XeO_4. In essence, this is a five-step algorithm.

1. Assume 100 grams of the compound.
2. Convert percent-by-weight data into grams of each element.
3. Calculate the number of moles of each element.
4. Calculate the ratio of the moles of each element.
5. Convert the answer to the simplest whole-number ratio, if necessary.

But what happens when we take out the hint that tells the students how to start this algorithm? Consider the following question:

9.33 g of copper metal was allowed to react with an excess of chlorine and it was found that 14.6 g of a compound of copper and chlorine were formed. What is the empirical formula of this compound? (Carter, et al., 1987, p. 653)

If you apply the concept of M-demand (Case, 1972; Pascual-Leone, 1970; Scardamalia, 1977) to this question, it has one, or at most two, more steps than the previous question. In theory, the known weight of copper (9.33 g) and chlorine (14.6 g - 9.33 g) in the sample could be converted into the percent by weight of these elements (63.9% Cu and 36.1% Cl). From that point, the algorithm for doing empirical formula calculations can be used intact.

But that isn't how either students or their instructors go about solving this problem. They seldom use the hint that this is an empirical formula question to construct a familiar problem (63.9% Cu and 36.1% Cl), which can be solved algorithmically. They use a totally different approach to the problem.

Algorithms are still used, but they involve much smaller chunks of information. Instead of a five-step algorithm, they use simpler algorithms, which automate individual steps in the calculation, such as converting from grams to moles.

ARCHISTIC VERSUS ANARCHISTIC APPROACHES TO PROBLEM SOLVING

From the beginning of our work on problem solving in chemistry, it was apparent that there was little similarity between the strategies our expert problem solvers used to solve problems that were novel to them and the solutions to these problems presented in the instructor's manuals that accompanied the textbooks from which the problems were taken.

As Herron (1990) has described it,

This difference between the problem-solving performance of experts and textbook solutions is significant because the examples must convey to the students an unrealistic idea about how problems are actually attacked. The examples provide no indication of the false starts, dead ends, and illogical attempts that characterize problem solving in its early stages, nor do they reveal the substantial time and effort expended to construct a useful representation of a problem before the systematic solution shown in examples is possible. (p. 35)

If you will allow me to coin a word — which I do reluctantly — I would like to describe these textbooks solutions as **archistic**.

The textbook solutions are perfectly logical sequences of steps that are strung together in a linear fashion from the initial information directly to the solution. They are perfect examples of how exercises would be worked by an individual who has many years of experience with similar tasks. They have little — if any — similarity, however, to the **anarchistic** approach experts use when they solve problems. (I owe a debt of gratitude to Lochhead (1979), who first described an anarchistic approach to teaching problem solving, which enabled me to recognize the role it plays in *doing* problem solving.)

Before I am accused of promoting the theory that all forms of government are oppressive and undesirable, let me remind you of another definition of anarchism: lacking order or control. In order to introduce an anarchistic model of problem solving, I must first comment on more established models.

STAGE MODELS FOR PROBLEM SOLVING

Polya (1945) was the first, but by no means the last, to propose a model of problem solving that involves stages, such as:

1. Understand the problem
2. Devise a plan
3. Carry out the plan
4. Look back

Our work has repeatedly shown the validity of this model for understanding how experts solve exercises. But it suggests that essentially all of the activities I would define as problem solving occur during the first stage.

Consider the following question:

A sample of a compound of xenon and fluorine was confined in a bulb with a pressure of 24 torr. Hydrogen was added to the bulb until the pressure was 96 torr. Passage of an electric spark through the mixture produced Xe and HF. After the HF was removed by reaction with solid KOH, the final pressure of xenon and unreacted hydrogen in the bulb was 48 torr. What is the empirical formula of the xenon fluoride in the original sample? (Holtzclaw, Robinson, & Nebergall, 1984, p. 278)

If your knowledge of chemistry is rusty, let me remind you that the partial pressure of each gas in this question is directly proportional to the number of moles of gas particles in the sample. Try to solve this problem before you continue reading.

Did you use Polya's four-stage model? Did you start by constructing an understanding of the problem? Did you then devise a plan, or a sequence of steps for solving the problem, before you carried out the plan?

This question should be a problem for virtually everyone who reads this chapter. As you reflect on your experience with this question, I believe you will conclude that you didn't fully understand the problem until you solved it. Furthermore, I doubt that you went through a stage in which you designed a sequence of steps that would lead to the solution before you carried out these steps.

I believe that Polya's stage model of problem solving, and its numerous archistic descendants, are better models of what happens when people work exercises or familiar problems. It has little to do with what happens when they solve problems.

AN ANARCHISTIC MODEL OF PROBLEM SOLVING

Over the last four years, I have been refining a model of what expert problem solvers do when they work problems, which is based on a model first proposed by Grayson Wheatley (1984).

1. Read the problem.
2. Now read the problem again.
3. Write down what you hope is the relevant information.
4. Draw a picture, make a list, or write an equation or formula to help you begin to understand the problem.
5. Try something.
6. Try something else.
7. See where this gets you.
8. Read the problem again.
9. Try something else.
10. See where this gets you.
11. Test intermediate results to see whether you are making any progress toward an answer.
12. Read the problem again.
13. When appropriate, strike your forehead and say, "Son of a ..."
14. Write down *an* answer (not necessarily *the* answer).
15. Test the answer to see if it makes sense.
16. Start over if you have to, celebrate if you don't.

When this model was proposed at a seminar in the chemistry department at Purdue, one of my colleagues summarily rejected it. He argued that this is what we do when we do research and stated that we can't expect students to approach problem solving the same way. I disagree.

The model of problem solving outlined above shares many of the characteristics that makes "science . . . an essentially anarchistic enterprise" (Feyerabend, 1975, p. 9). Whereas exercises are often worked in a linear, forward-chaining, rational manner, this model of problem solving is cyclic, reflective, and might even appear irrational to anyone watching us use it.

IMPORTANCE OF DIFFERENTIATING BETWEEN
EXERCISES AND PROBLEMS

Why do I place so much emphasis on the difference between exercises and problems? In chemistry, we are already doing a fairly good job of teaching students to work exercises. We introduce them to certain classes of problems, such as the empirical formula calculations described earlier. We then lead them through enough similar questions until the successful ones build an algorithm for doing these calculations. As a result of this instruction, we have produced good exercise solvers. We are much less successful, however, at teaching them to be good problem solvers.

Some of my more pessimistic colleagues believe that the only realistic goal we can attain is have our students work more and more complex exercises. I pray they are wrong. I believe that the ultimate goal of the research in this area is to improve the problem-solving skills of our students.

Unfortunately, when my colleagues in chemistry read the problem-solving literature, they invariably walk away with models that suggest students should be able to work problems much the same way they work exercises. They therefore present beautiful algorithmic approaches to their students for working problems. When students fail at problem solving with these techniques, they conclude that their students are either stupid or lazy.

Ever since I began teaching, I have listened to colleagues bemoan the fact that beginning students seem to be able to handle one-step questions, or perhaps two-step questions, but not questions that are more complex. I think I understand why.

Several years ago, the students in my course were assigned the following question:

> A sample of indium bromide weighing 0.100 g reacts with silver nitrate, $AgNO_3$, giving indium nitrate and 0.159 g of AgBr. Determine the empirical formula of indium bromide. (Holtzclaw, et al., 1984, p. 54)

This is a difficult question, which is a problem for all of my students and many of the teaching assistants as well. In virtually every recitation section, the students asked the Teaching Assistant (TA) to do this problem. I noticed that the essentially all of the TA's told their students that the problem could be worked more or less like this:

> Start by converting grams of AgBr into moles of AgBr. Convert moles of AgBr into moles of Br and then convert moles of Br into grams of Br. Subtract grams of Br from grams of indium bromide to give grams of In. Convert grams of In into moles of In. Then divide moles of Br by moles of In to get the empirical formula of the compound.

During the next staff meeting, I asked the TA's to stop lying to the students. I told them that the technique for solving this problem they had presented to their students had little if anything to do with the process they had used to solve the problem for the first time. I argued that they had confused the process used to solve exercises with the process used to solve problems. Finally, I suggested that the description given above was an algorithm for solving similar questions, which they had constructed *after* they had solved this problem. Thus, it wasn't surprising when the students reported to me that they felt discouraged, because they weren't capable of solving the problem the way their TA's did.

WHAT IS THE EFFECT OF NOT DISTINGUISHING BETWEEN EXERCISES AND PROBLEMS?

In a study of the role of beliefs in problem solving in chemistry, Carter (1987) reported her experience as a teaching assistant in a junior-level physical chemistry course. Her students found physical chemistry to be a difficult or frustrating obstacle on the way to engineering, chemistry, or biology degrees. She and her fellow TA's, on the other hand, were frustrated with the students. They felt that the students lacked basic problem-solving skills, in spite of their strong mathematical backgrounds. While they were adept at using algorithms and manipulating numbers, they seemed unable to apply their skills with basic chemical concepts when presented with a novel problem. Few seemed to see the need to develop complete, coherent representations of problems, and the equations they memorized seemed to be disconnected bits of information.

The main source of the TA's frustration, however, was that the students saw nothing wrong with this. Physical chemistry was supposed to be hard; it wasn't supposed to make sense. Because the students believed that they couldn't be expected to actually understand physical chemistry, they dealt with the material accordingly. They memorized equations, and worked examples of the same problem type over and over again, with little concern as to why that particular pattern or method worked, or why it did not.

The students' attempts to treat physical chemistry in terms of exercises, which can be handled by memorizing equations and algorithms for doing calculations, inevitably led to frustration on the part of both the students and their instructors. The students were frustrated because they weren't successful at this task. Their instructors were frustrated because the students weren't behaving properly.

IMPLICATIONS OF THE ANARCHISTIC MODEL OF PROBLEM SOLVING

The model proposed in this chapter has helped me understand many of the observations made during the 17 years I've taught general chemistry. I can understand why so many beginning students have difficulty learning how to do even the simplest stoichiometry calculations, such as the following:

How much carbon dioxide is produced when 10.0 grams of sugar in the form of sucrose ($C_{12}H_{22}O_{11}$) react with excess oxygen?

$$C_{12}H_{22}O_{11}(aq) + 12\ O_2(g) \longrightarrow 12\ CO_2(g) + 11\ H_2O(l)$$

This task, which is a simple exercise for their instructors, is a problem to them. Until they stumble on the answer to enough problems of this nature to build their own algorithm for working them, watching their instructor do the calculation as an exercise isn't going to be sufficient. (An expert watching them approach these problems might consider their work to be "disorganized," or even "irrational," because it differed so much from the approach the expert would take. If the expert is the student's instructor, he or she might be tempted to intervene, to show the student the "correct" way of obtaining the answer. While this might make the instructor feel good, it doesn't necessarily help the student.)

This model has also helped me understand why so many students who successfully build an algorithm to do the calculation given above fail when they encounter the following limiting reagent question, which appears on the surface to be similar.

How much carbon dioxide is produced when 10.0 grams of sugar in the form of sucrose ($C_{12}H_{22}O_{11}$) react with 10.0 grams of oxygen?

$$C_{12}H_{22}O_{11}(aq) + 12\ O_2(g) \longrightarrow 12\ CO_2(g) + 11\ H_2O(l)$$

In order to answer this question, one would have to calculate the amount of carbon dioxide that could be obtained from 10.0 grams of sucrose. But then one would have to recognize that there might not be enough oxygen to consume all of the sugar. One might then calculate the amount of oxygen that would be needed and see if there is enough. Alternatively, one could calculate the amount of carbon dioxide that could be obtained from 10.0 grams of oxygen. Then, one would have to compare the results of these calculations, and decide which reagent is present in excess and which reagent limits the extent of reaction. Only then can the amount of CO_2 be predicted. In other words, there is more to solving this problem than applying stoichiometry algorithms in the correct order (Bodner & McMillen, 1986).

IMPLICATIONS OF THE ANARCHISTIC MODEL FOR TEACHING

This model brings into question some of the techniques used to teach chemistry at present. As Herron and Greenbowe (1986) note:

Virtually all problem-solving activities in standard courses focus on problems for which an algorithmic solution has been taught. ... Our research reveals that expert problem solvers never follow such direct paths when confronted with novel tasks, and most problems in chemistry are novel to the students in the course. We believe that we must give far more attention to how experienced problem solvers go about making sense out of problems encountered for the first time. (p. 530)

The model also provides a hint as to how to improve the teaching of chemistry.

Herron and Greenbowe continue:

> Expert problem solvers make use of a number of general strategies (heuristics) as they interpret, represent, and solve problems. Trial and error, thinking of the problem in terms of the physical system discussed, solving a special case, solving a simple problem that seems related to a difficult problem, ... breaking the problem into parts, substituting numbers for variables, drawing diagrams to represent molecules and atoms, and checking interim or final results against other information ... are common strategies used by successful problem solvers. Although teachers frequently use these strategies, little attention is given to teaching these strategies to students. (p. 530)

Is it possible to improve the problem-solving performance of beginning chemistry students? Frank (1985) constructed a study to see if intervention during recitation sections could achieve this result. Students in the experimental section were encouraged to ask questions such as:

> What is the unknown? What are the conditions? What do these substances look like? How do the atoms and molecules involved here interact? How could you symbolize what you see? (p. 71 - 88)

Students in the experimental group outscored the control students on class exams. They formed more generalizable representations, were more persistent, and evaluated their work more frequently than control students. They also worked toward an inappropriate goal more often, perhaps as a result of increased confidence — these students worked toward an inappropriate goal under conditions where students in the control group either gave up or worked toward no goal at all.

When you consider that the intervention in Frank's study occurred only in recitation, these results are promising. They should be viewed with care, however. One of the instructors in this study made the following observations.

> Some of my students seemed to enjoy group work and the emphasis on a few general principles. Others, however, were frustrated or threatened by the non-traditional approach. They believed chemistry teachers were supposed to tell them the answers or show them how to work problems. Since they were not told which equations to memorize, or "the" method of working each problem, they could not be expected to succeed on the exams. A conflict existed between my beliefs about the nature of learning chemistry and what my students believed . . . a conflict only compounded by the gap between my goal of improving their problem-solving skills and their goals, which often consisted of particular course grades. (Carter, 1987, p. 1.).

REFERENCES

Bodner, G. M. (1986). Constructivism: A theory of knowledge. *Journal of Chemical Education, 63*, 873-878.

Bodner, G. M. (1987). The role of algorithms in teaching problem solving. *Journal of Chemical Education, 64*, 513-514.

Bodner, G. M., & McMillen, T. L. B. (1986). Cognitive restructuring as an early stage in problem solving. *Journal of Research in Science Teaching, 23*, 727-737.

Carroll, L. (1935). *Through the looking glass and what Alice found there*, Chapter 6. NY: The Limited Editions Club.

Carter, C. S. (1987). *The role of beliefs in general chemistry problem solving*. Unpublished doctoral dissertation, Purdue University, West Lafayette, IN.

Carter, C. S., LaRussa, M. A., & Bodner, G. M. (1987). A study of two measures of spatial ability as predictors of success in different levels of general chemistry. *Journal of Research in Science Teaching, 24*, 645-657.

Case, R. (1972). Validation of a neo-Piagetian mental capacity construct. *Journal of Experimental Child Psychology, 14*, 287-302.

Ehrlich, E., Flexner, S. B., Carruth, G., & Hawkins, J. M. (1980). *Oxford American Dictionary*. Oxford: Oxford University Press.

Feyerabend, P. (1975). *Against method: Outline of an anarchistic theory of knowledge*. Thetford, Norfolk: Thetford Press Limited.

Frank, D. V. (1985). *Implementing instruction to improve the problem-solving abilities of general chemistry students*. Unpublished doctoral dissertation, Purdue University, West Lafayette, IN.

Hayes, J. (1980). *The complete problem solver*. Philadelphia: The Franklin Institute.

Herron, J. D. (1990). Research in chemical education: Results and directions. In M. Gardner, J. G. Greeno, F. Reif, A. H. Schoenfeld, A. A. diSessa, & E. Stage (Eds.), *Toward a scientific practice of science education* (pp. 31-54). Hillsdale, NJ: Erlbaum.

Herron, J. D., & Greenbowe, T. J. (1986). What can we do about Sue?: A case study of competence. *Journal of Chemical Education, 63*, 528-531.

Holtzclaw, H. F., Robinson, W. R., & Nebergall, W. H. (1984). *General chemistry* (7th ed.). Lexington, MA, DC Heath.

Johnstone, A. H., & El-Banna, H. (1986). Capacities, demands and processes — a predictive model for science education. *Education in Chemistry, 23*(3), 80-84.

Lochhead, J. (1979, April). *An anarchistic approach to teaching problem solving methods*. Paper presented at the annual meeting of the American Educational Research Association, San Francisco, CA.

Pascual-Leone, J. (1970). A mathematical model for the transition rule in Piaget's developmental stages. *Acta Psychologica, 32*, 301-345.

Patel, V. L., & Groen, G. (1988, April). *Toward a unified theory of problem solving: A view from medicine*. Paper presented at the annual meeting of the American Educational Research Association, New Orleans, LA.

Polya, G. (1945). *How to solve it: A new aspect of mathematical method*. Princeton, NJ: Princeton University Press.

Scardamalia, M. (1977). Information processing capacity and the problem of horizontal *decalage*: A demonstration using combination reasoning tasks. *Child Development, 48*, 28-37.

Smith, M. U. (1988, April). *Toward a unified theory of problem solving: A view from biology*. Paper presented at the annual meeting of the American Educational Research Association, New Orleans, LA.

Wheatley, G. H. (1984). *Problem solving in school mathematics* (MEPS Technical Report No. 84.01) West Lafayette, IN: Purdue University, School Mathematics and Science Center.

"It's unified and it's a theory, but it's not the unified theory we've all been looking for."

3

A VIEW FROM MEDICINE

Guy J. Groen
Vimla L. Patel
McGill University

The development of theories of problem solving in educational contexts can be approached from two directions, frequently achieving different results. One approach is to directly examine the teaching of problem solving in practical situations and then to generalize from the task and domain specificity that inevitably arises. The second approach is to begin with a general theory and discover how it applies in specific domains. These two approaches tend to yield different results because the level of specificity tends to determine what is easy or hard to examine. Thus, in the first approach, a theory based on arithmetic may focus on quite different issues from a theory based on geometry. This issue is particularly exacerbated in medicine because the domain is organized into a complex hierarchy of specialties and subspecialties which are all connected to certain types of general knowledge that is generally assumed to be required of all practitioners. For medicine, therefore, it is useful to consider the second approach.

There exists in the literature of cognitive psychology a theory of problem solving for which a considerable amount of generality has been claimed. This is the approach developed primarily by Herbert Simon, Alan Newell, and their colleagues at Carnegie Mellon University (Ericsson & Simon, 1984; Greeno & Simon, 1988; Newell & Simon, 1972). Its most recent incarnation, in Newell's SOAR system

(Newell, 1988), includes a highly developed theory of learning as well as perform-ance.

An important component of this general theoretical approach is a theory of expert reasoning that is based on three basic notions. The first is that experts develop highly efficient ways of representing in working memory the information given in a problem-solving situation. The second notion is that knowledge in long term memory is representable as a set of production rules that specify what action is to be performed when a specific situation arises. Expertise is determined by the existence of a large number of highly domain-specific rules of this type. The third notion is the distinction between strong and weak methods. Strong methods are heuristic strategies that use the knowledge base to limit the amount of searching that is required. Thus if a problem is familiar to the expert, a set of rules can be applied that lead directly to a solution from the facts given in the problem statement or observed in a problem situation. This process is usually called forward chaining or forward reasoning because of the implied directionality (from facts to a solution). In contrast, weak methods are heuristics that do not rely on the existence of a developed knowledge base. While there are many such methods ranging from brute force exhaustive search to sophisticated hypothetico-deductive reasoning, they all rely on some form of what might be termed reality assessment in which the validity of a hypothesis or the attainment of a goal is checked against the given facts, or an attempt is made to obtain further facts that are not immediately evident. In other words, they involve the use of backward rather than forward reasoning. It is important to note that this backward reasoning can also be used by experts, especially when their knowledge base is inadequate to reach a satisfactory solution immediately (as may well be the case in most non-routine situations).

As we have discussed at length elsewhere (Patel & Groen, in press), the validity or plausibility of large scale cognitive theories such as this cannot be directly established by a few experiments or even by empirical evidence alone. Rather, it depends on convergent evidence from a number of sources. Thus, much of the support for the Newell-Simon theory comes from its widespread use in cognitive psychology as a means of describing problem-solving processes and its adoption in artificial intelligence as the basic methodology for the development of expert systems. However, this theory does lead one to expect certain empirical phenom-ena, the absence of which would cast serious doubts on the theory's plausibility. One such prediction is the existence of knowledge-dependent chunking strategies resulting in enhanced recall. Another is the use of forward reasoning in correctly solving at least some routine problems. The critical issue is to show the existence rather than the generality of the phenomenon. These phenomena have, in fact, been demonstrated, though in a limited range of domains. Many experiments have been performed that demonstrate the enhanced recall phenomenon, primarily in studies of expert-novice differences in games such as chess and bridge (Charness, 1989; Chase & Simon, 1973; deGroot, 1965). There is less evidence for the existence of forward reasoning, which has been demonstrated primarily in a few studies of routine problem solving in physics (Larkin, McDermott, Simon, & Simon, 1980; Simon & Simon, 1978). There is, however, considerable converging evidence from the area of expert systems where expert protocols are routinely gathered and used as a basis for system design.

The purpose of this paper is to examine the applicability of this general theory to the field of medical education. We will consider three specific issues. The first is the extent to which the basic empirical phenomena of forward reasoning and enhanced recall appear. The second issue is to consider the applicability of this kind of theory of expert reasoning to the problem solving of the individual who is less than expert. The third issue is whether or not the theory has any relevance to practical issues of teaching and evaluation.

MEDICAL EDUCATION

In the 1960s a movement in medical education arose that attempted to apply discovery learning techniques to the training of medical students. This curriculum design was advocated under the rubric of "problem-based learning." The experience in medicine was similar to experience with techniques of this kind in other areas. Despite an intuitive face validity, it was difficult to verify the success of the approach through the use of primitive outcome measures. The issues were more subtle and ambiguous than those assessed by such measures. It was necessary to develop a more theoretical approach in order to tie together the seemingly contradictory results that were obtained.

One possibility was to introduce at least some elements of modern cognitive psychology, as was done in a seminal book by Elstein, Shulman, and Sprafka (1978). This work, however, may have raised more problems than it solved, especially in relationship to mainstream cognitive psychology. One such problem, which formed the main motivation of our own work, was a certain lack of consistency between the general view of expertise in medicine and that which had begun to develop in other areas such as physics. Whereas the major emphasis in such areas was on the role of forward or inductive reasoning, Elstein et al. emphasized the role of backward reasoning and the use of hypothetico-deductive approaches. Also they found no differences between experts and novices except in the extent of the knowledge base. This lack of consistency was reinforced by later research conducted by others. Having been highly influenced by the work of deGroot, Elstein et al. attempted to extend into the area of medicine the kinds of studies being conducted by Chase and Simon (1973) which were essentially more carefully controlled replications of deGroot's research. A number of studies (e.g., Norman, Jacoby, Feightner, & Campbell, 1979) were conducted that examined expert-novice differences in the free recall of clinical cases, utilizing dependent measures that roughly parallel those used by Chase and Simon. Recall was measured in terms of the number of sentences accurately reproduced, and chunk size was estimated in terms of the number of words between pauses. However, the apparently paradoxical result emerged that, while there was a difference in the ability to chunk, there was no difference between experts and novices in the overall level of recall.

COMPREHENSION AND EXPLANATION OF CLINICAL CASES

In this section, we briefly summarize our own research. The reader is referred to Groen and Patel (1988) and Patel and Groen (in press) for more extensive treatments of the basic empirical and theoretical issues. This research was originally motivated by the possibility that the anomalies in the results of the free recall experiments might be due to an inadequate method of scoring the recall protocols that relied exclusively on surface structure features of the case presentation. An alternative was to make use of the propositional techniques developed by Kintsch (1974) and by Frederiksen (1975) to explore the possibility that the proposition might provide a more malleable means of defining unit recall than the chunk when dealing with complex verbal data. In a sequence of experiments (Patel, Groen, & Frederiksen, 1986) using a standard free-recall paradigm and a method of recall-inference analysis developed by Frederiksen (1981), we found differences between experts and novices in free recall that were consistent with results such as those obtained by Chase and Simon. Experts remembered more of the material relevant to the actual diagnosis of the case, although in the form of "inferences" (minor changes that preserved the semantics of the proposition) rather than verbatim recall.

These results led us to believe that it might be possible to discover evidence for forward reasoning in the diagnosis of clinical cases. We soon found that we were unable to use a straightforward problem-solving paradigm because standard "thinking aloud" techniques invariably yielded extremely sparse protocols. As a result we used a paradigm that we call diagnostic explanation, in which subjects were requested to explain the pathophysiology, or causal patterns, underlying a clinical case. Patel and Groen (1986) obtained results using these paradigms that were indeed consistent with patterns of expert reasoning in other areas. When their diagnoses were accurate, expert physicians explained routine problems of medical diagnosis by means of an inductive process of pure forward reasoning (from data to diagnosis) as opposed to a deductive process of backward reasoning (from diagnosis to data). With incomplete diagnoses, a mixture of forward and backward reasoning was used. It is important to note that these results were strong in the sense that all subjects with correct diagnoses used pure forward reasoning whereas it was used by no subjects with incomplete or inaccurate diagnoses.

More recently, we have been extending our research to the investigation of less-than-expert reasoning (Patel, Groen, & Arocha, in press). This has involved subjects in three broad categories: subexperts (experts solving problems outside their domain of expertise), intermediates (students who have received some instruction in the domain), and novices (students with negligible knowledge of the domain). In general, our ability to obtain coherent results has depended on the level of expertise of our subjects. Subexperts usually make incomplete or inaccurate diagnoses. Their explanations tend to resemble the reasoning of an expert in the domain who reaches an incomplete diagnosis except that there is a marked tendency for the subexperts to focus on aspects related to their own specialties. As we proceed backward, as it were, toward the novice level, however, the protocols begin to show more and more between-subject variability, which makes it difficult if not impossible to compare protocols in a systematic fashion. We have uncovered two phenomena at these lower levels. The first is that intermediates recall more irrelevant material than novices or experts. This can be interpreted as implying that intermediates tend to utilize recently learned information that has not been adequately integrated into their knowledge base. This lack of integration leads to the inappropriate application of the recently acquired information and, thus, to less successful performance. The second phenomenon is more specific. In an attempt to obtain more coherent protocols, students were presented with basic science information in addition to the clinical case that they were asked to explain. In these experiments, subjects only utilized these basic science facts in their diagnostic explanations if that information was presented after the clinical case. In other words, the clinical problem could not be embedded into the basic science context. Rather, the basic science had to be embedded within the clinical context.

A UNIFIED THEORY OF EXPERTISE AND ITS LIMITATIONS

These results suggest that it is possible to establish a theory of expertise that applies across most domains. In broad outline, experts readily comprehend new information and integrate it into their existing knowledge base. This results in an enhanced ability to recall and chunk information. It also results in the ability to cope with routine situations rapidly and efficiently by the use of forward reasoning through a limited search space. Differences between domains may reflect primarily the complexity of the situations and the predominant mode of responding to them. In the aspects of medicine with which we have been concerned the situations are very complex, and a large part of the expert's task is to filter out irrelevant detail. This probably explains the expert's tendency to recall only the relevant information. The response modes are highly verbal, which explains why many of the similarities with other domains only become apparent through the use of propositional representations to make explicit the underlying pattern of results. Because of the pressures inherent in medical practice, the reasoning strategies are highly automated. This fact may explain the necessity of using an explanation task rather than the more direct problem-solving tasks used in other domains, for obtaining adequate protocols.

Unfortunately this coherence and generality breaks down as the situations become non-routine and the level of expertise decreases. The theory of Newell and Simon (1972) suggests that strong methods are replaced by weak methods as the relevant knowledge base decreases or the level of uncertainty increases. This proposition is supported by the evidence cited above in which an absence of forward reasoning by experts when explaining inaccurate or incomplete diagnoses was observed. However, the role and nature of weak methods in even expert reasoning is little understood and somewhat controversial (e.g., Newell, 1988). In our own research, we have obtained some evidence of backward reasoning in more complex, though still routine, clinical cases when experts explain facts that are not directly relevant to the main diagnosis (Patel, Groen, & Arocha, in press).

From an educational point of view, this lack of understanding of the nature of weak methods is important because the students encountered in most instructional situations are novices or intermediates rather than experts or subexperts. For a number of years, it was widely assumed that it was possible to accelerate learning by teaching students the rules, or modes of reasoning, that experts used. However, a considerable amount of research (especially in the area of intelligent tutoring systems) has led to the conclusion that it is impossible for students to learn these expert approaches directly. Apart from the limitations inherent in a purely rule-based approach, there appears to be no logical connection between models of novices and models of experts. Novice rules do not map onto expert rules. Moreover, this lack of relationship cannot be explained solely on a basis of bugs and misconceptions. Small sets of expert rules can sometimes be taught to a beginner, but they form isolated segments of knowledge that are not connected to anything else and are seldom retained for any length of time.

These observations imply that a cognitive theory will only be applicable to practical issues of education if it incorporates a theory of novice reasoning. An expert theory may be valuable for establishing norms or objectives, but it cannot be applied to instruction or even realistic diagnosis and testing (unless the goal of the test is to establish how close a student is to the expert level, as might be the case in a certification exam). Unfortunately, a theory of novice reasoning that is even remotely comparable in precision and generality to the current theory of expert reasoning does not exist at this time. It is important to note that this is not a problem within medical education alone. It exists in all of cognitive science.

TOWARD A THEORY OF NOVICE AND INTERMEDIATE REASONING

To begin, it is important to clarify some terminology. The notion of a novice or intermediate makes sense only in the context of a specific domain of expertise. An expert is someone who has demonstrable mastery of the domain. It should be noted that this implies a judgment based on comparison against a criterion. For example, it is possible to use official ratings in the case of chess or board certifications in the case of medicine. However, there are many domains in which such clear criteria are lacking. In the light of what we now know about expertise, it is tempting to define an expert as someone who is always correct on routine problems and solves them by means of forward reasoning. In that case, the domain of expertise can be defined in terms of frequently encountered situations.

A novice is a student with no self-taught knowledge and no training (formal or informal) in the domain.   An intermediate is anyone whose knowledge of the domain is in between that of the novice and the expert. This range is so vast that it is important to be more precise, a task that is very difficult because the area has been so little studied. Our own research indicates that it is important to make a distinction between subexperts (those who have expertise in a closely related domain) and intermediates in general. At the other end of the scale, it seems important to develop a means of distinguishing between intermediates and beginners, possibly on the basis of time devoted to learning the domain, or whether or not appropriate courses have been passed. Our research indicates that, if these two categories are excluded, then a distinctive developmental phenomenon emerges. On certain outcome measures primarily associated with comprehension, intermediates perform more poorly than either experts or novices.

Such phenomena may seem surprising in a context of adult learning, but are quite common in the literature of developmental psychology. Indeed, there are striking parallels between important notions in developmental psychology and research on expert-novice differences. In particular the theory of expert-novice differences resembles a theory of developmental stages. In fact, in some of the tasks Piaget studies, children in the stage of formal operations might be viewed as experts whereas children in the stage of concrete operations might be viewed as intermediates. The non-monotonicity phenomena encountered in the developmental literature usually emerge as result of an empirical test of some kind of stage theory, with pre-adolescent children performing more poorly than either adolescents or younger children. There is also some evidence (Groen & Kieran 1982) that Piaget himself viewed concrete operations as a buggy stage where children made reasoning errors that could not be explained on the basis of a smooth developmental transition. It is therefore not surprising to see the same phenomenon emerge with adult intermediates.

Such parallels suggest a possible approach to the development of a unified theory of novice and intermediate reasoning that takes advantage of both the vast empirical literature on cognitive development and the existence of a well-developed theory of adult expertise. The theory has two components. The first is to view novices as entering a domain with certain kinds of expertise based on commonsense knowledge and everyday experience and to view learning as something that either builds upon or abandons this expertise. Similarly, intermediates may be viewed as individuals with expertise in domains that are closely related but not identical to the domain they are learning. In medicine, for example, intermediates have developed a considerable amount of expertise in the basic sciences but very little in the clinical areas. There is evidence that the performance decrements mentioned above may be due to an excessive reliance on basic science knowledge.

The second component is to acknowledge that the resemblance of the theory of expert-novice differences to developmental stage theories may imply that it shares some of their weaknesses. Apart from the existence of a detailed process theory at the expert level, there is neither more nor less to be gained from expert-novice comparisons than there is from distinctions between concrete and formal operations, for example. It is insufficient to simply specify the processes typically used at the novice, intermediate, and expert levels. What is needed most of all is the development of detailed process theories that specify the transition mechanisms that allow the student to progress from one level to another. In developmental psychology, the analogous task has turned out to be very difficult and has raised some profound epistemological problems. There is every likelihood that exactly the same problems will soon be encountered in the study of adult cognition.

EXPLANATION AND LEARNING

We conclude this chapter by discussing some ramifications of the diagnostic explanation paradigm that we have been using. With the exception of research stemming from notions of mental models, explanation tasks are not frequently seen in studies of adult cognition. They are quite common, however, in the developmental literature where they are used as a means of assessing a child's degree of understanding of a concept. In the case of Piaget's notion of *abstraction reflechissant*, explanation to one's own self achieves the status of a major theoretical construct, being viewed as a mechanism that enables major developmental changes.

In the case of our paradigm, we find that forward reasoning is associated with successful performance and tends to disappear when a subject is uncertain or unsuccessful. This observation can be generalized in terms of Newell's distinction between strong methods (of which forward reasoning is an indicator) and weak methods (of which backward reasoning is an indicator). The former might be viewed as efficient ways of utilizing existing knowledge whereas the latter are less efficient ways of proceeding when knowledge is inadequate for utilizing the more efficient strong methods. Newell presents an elaborate typology of weak methods, some of which are simply heuristics for achieving an approximate solution. Others, however, are means of attaining new knowledge. The presence of backward reasoning in an explanation paradigm may therefore imply that the subject is attempting to learn something new from the explanation.

This implication is important for understanding the performance of novices and intermediates. Even though a novice's explanation may be riddled with bugs and misconceptions, their harmful effects may be dependent on the direction of reasoning. If it is forward, then the subject is likely to view his or her existing knowledge base as adequate. This implies that misconceptions will be long-lasting and difficult to eradicate. If it is backward, then the misconceptions may simply be a means to an end. In this case, these incorrect ideas might best be viewed as transient hypotheses which are later either refuted or modified in the light of experience to form the kernel of a more adequate explanation. With intermediates, the reason for errors does not lie with serious misconceptions as much as with an excessive use of irrelevant information. Once again, the fundamental issue may lie in how this information is being used. The use of forward reasoning may indicate a dogmatic reliance on existing knowledge. Backward reasoning may indicate that the subject is attempting to learn how to separate out the relevant from the irrelevant.

These implications suggest that an instructional emphasis on the importance of correct problem solving and the harmfulness of misconceptions may not be productive. The important part of learning may consist in testing and pondering the adequacy of one's explanations rather than achieving accurately implemented solution procedures. If this is so, then a greater instructional emphasis on explanation rather than problem solving might prove profitable. The "problem-based learning" we mentioned at the beginning of this paper might at least be supplemented by "explanation-based learning."

REFERENCES

Charness, N. (1989). Expertise in chess and bridge. In D. Klahr & K. Kotovsky (Eds.), *Complex information processing: The impact of Herbert A. Simon* (pp. 183-208). Hillsdale, NJ: Lawrence Erlbaum Associates.

Chase, W.G., & Simon, H.A. (1973). Perception in chess. *Cognitive Psychology, 1*, 55-81.

deGroot, A.D. (1965). *Thought and choice in chess.* The Hague: Mouton .

Elstein, A.S., Shulman, L.S., & Sprafka, S.A. (1978). *Medical problem solving: An analysis of clinical reasoning.* Cambridge, MA: Harvard University Press.

Ericsson, A., & Simon, H.A. (1984). *Protocol analysis: Verbal reports as data.* Cambridge, MA: MIT Press.

Frederiksen, C.H. (1975). Representing logical and semantic structure of knowledge acquired from discourse. *Cognitive Psychology, 7,* 371-458.

Frederiksen, C.H. (1981). Inferences in preschool children's conversations: A cognitive perspective. In J. Green & C. Wallat (Eds.), *Ethnography and language in educational settings.* Norwood, NJ: Ablex.

Greeno, J. G., & Simon, H. A. (1988). Problem solving and reasoning. In R.C. Atkinson, R. Hernstein, G. Lindsey, & R.D. Luce (Eds.), *Steven's handbook of experimental psychology.* New York: Wiley.

Groen, G.J., & Kieran, C. (1982). In search of Piagetian mathematics. In H. Ginsburg (Ed.), *The development of mathematical thinking* (pp. 351-374). New York: Academic.

Groen, G.J., & Patel, V.L. (1988). The relationship between comprehension and reasoning in medical expertise. In M. Chi, R. Glaser & M. Farr (Eds.), *The nature of expertise* (pp. 287-310). Hillsdale, NJ: Lawrence Erlbaum Associates.

Kintsch, W. (1974). *The representation of meaning in memory*. Hillsdale, NJ: Lawrence Erlbaum Associates.

Larkin, J., McDermott, J., Simon, D.P., & Simon, H.A. (1980). Expert and novice performances in solving physics problems. *Science, 208,* 1335-1342.

Newell, A., & Simon, H.A. (1972). *Human problem solving*. Englewood Cliffs, NJ:Prentice-Hall.

Newell, A. (1988, August). *Unified theory of problem solving*. Paper presented at the Tenth Annual Conference of the Cognitive Science Society. Montreal, Canada.

Norman, G.R., Jacoby, L.L., Feightner, J.W., & Campbell, G.J.M. (1979, November). Clinical experience and the structure of memory. *Proceedings of the 18th Conference for Research in Medical Education,* Washington, DC.

Patel, V.L. , & Groen, G.J. (1986). Knowledge based solution strategies in medical reasoning. *Cognitive Science, 10,* 91-116.

Patel, V.L., & Groen, G.J. (in press). The generality of medical expertise: A critical look. In A. Ericsson & J. Smith (Eds.), *Study of expertise: Prospects and limits*. Cambridge, MA: MIT Press.

Patel,V.L., Groen, G.J., & Arocha, J.F. (in press). Medical expertise as a function of task difficulty. *Memory and Cognition.*

Patel, V.L., Groen, G.J., & Frederiksen, C.H. (1986). Differences between students and physicians in memory for clinical cases. *Medical Education, 20,* 3-9.

Simon, D.P., & Simon, H.A. (1978). Individual differences in solving physics problems. In R. Siegler (Ed.), *Children's thinking: What develops?* (pp. 325 - 348) Hillsdale, NJ: Lawrence Erlbaum Associates.

4 A VIEW FROM PROGRAMMING

David N. Perkins
Steven Schwartz
Rebecca Simmons
Harvard University

INTRODUCTION

Like cognition of all sorts, effective problem solving poses profound and provocative puzzles about the relationship between the general and the particular. How, for instance, does one's general knowledge of a domain (for example, knowledge of Newton's laws in physics or FOR-NEXT loops in programming) inform the solving of a specific problem in that domain? To what extent does knowledge that cuts across domains, for example, general problem-solving heuristics and self-management techniques, inform the resolution of a specific problem?

Although these are important questions to ask, some might aver that contemporary cognitive science has gone a long way toward answering them already. Findings from the extensive research on expertise argue that good problem solving within a domain depends mostly on a large repertoire of highly "compiled" domain-specific schemata, what is sometimes called "local knowledge." General crosscutting methods — "weak methods," as they have been named — do not count for much. The question about the relation between general and local knowledge dissolves into the resolution that "local knowledge wins," accounting for nearly all the variance in effective problem solving (e.g., Chase & Simon, 1973; Chi, Glaser, & Rees, 1982; Glaser, 1984; Larkin, McDermott, Simon, & Simon, 1980).

This chapter addresses the relation between general and local knowledge in the case of computer programming, with occasional forays into other domains. It urges that a strong local knowledge position seriously misconceives the importance of general knowledge and leads us away from efforts to map the manner in which general knowledge *is* brought to bear in dealing with the particulars of a knowledge domain.

Before considering the particulars of programming, we would like to address the limits of the local knowledge position and what questions arise in consequence. To be sure, the research on expertise shows that expert performance on typical domain problems is dominated by local knowledge and demonstrates clearly that novices often fail to solve problems for lack of such knowledge. However, such results in themselves do not demonstrate that local knowledge is the overwhelmingly dominant independent variable in problem solving because they reflect a restricted sample: *typical* domain problems. What if one instead asked experts to address problems that are somewhat atypical but plainly within the domain? One might even pick problems that are not highly technical but that simply stand off to one side of conventional textbook problems. Under such conditions, experts can be seen evoking all sorts of general knowledge together with local knowledge (e.g., Clement, 1982, in press).

The expertise literature paints a picture of good problem solving as highly domain centered. In contrast, the above remarks suggest what we call a "fractal image" of thinking. While this metaphor will be developed in the concluding section, the general idea is straightforward. At least when problems depart from the conventional, knowledge at all levels of generality from the very local to the very global is likely to figure in the problem solver's effort. The question becomes: How can one understand the collaborative relationship?

In pursuing this inquiry we turn to investigations about computer programming and its pedagogy conducted by our team over the past five years. In various ways, the relationships between general and particular knowledge have been examined. After a look at several facets of this research, we conclude by returning to the fractal image and suggesting several overarching principles concerning the relationship between general and local knowledge in problem solving.

LOCAL KNOWLEDGE IN PROGRAMMING
AND THE PROBLEM OF ACCESS

As a point of logic, it's clear that merely "having" local knowledge is not sufficient for its good use. Indeed, the research on expertise demonstrates that experts not only have an extensive domain-specific knowledge base, but deploy it smoothly, almost reflexively (Chase & Simon, 1973; Chi et al., 1982; Glaser, 1984;

Larkin et al., 1980). Consequently, a question arises whether in novices there is a significant gap between "having" and "using" local knowledge. It might be that, as students acquire local knowledge, they also acquire the good use of it, so that expert use of knowledge develops more or less smoothly with the accretion of knowledge. On the other hand, it might instead be that students acquire considerable domain-specific knowledge that is largely unusable, and it cannot be effectively accessed to deal with particular problems.

Empirical research in our group has disclosed that there is indeed a substantial gap between what students know about programming and what they can do. In clinical studies with high school BASIC students we found that many errors students committed that were seemingly due to lack of knowledge of the language could not be attributed to knowledge simply missing from their memories (Perkins & Martin, 1986; Perkins, Martin, & Farady, 1986). Nor was it that students lacked the knowledge in question, once reminded of it. Rather, with minimal prompting, students often were able to apply knowledge that had previously appeared to be absent.

As an example, consider the case of a first-semester BASIC student who was trying to write a program to print out a square of stars (5 rows by 5 columns of asterisks). He had coded two nested FOR-loops, but his program resulted in a horizontal row of 25 stars on the screen rather than the specified square. He examined his code, but was unable to come up with a solution. It appeared that the student lacked the proper knowledge to complete the task.

However, when prompted by the experimenter with "What do you need to do?", the student was able to define the next step: Make the stars into a square. He then went on to retrieve the right command for accomplishing this task, inserting a blank PRINT line after the first NEXT statement in order to force carriage returns that would produce rows of stars. In this case, the experimenter's general prompt led the student to define his problem and then access the appropriate programming knowledge to provide the solution. This example is fairly typical of many in our clinical interviews where scaffolding by the experimenter revealed a surprising amount of unaccessed student knowledge.

In another example, a student was working on a simple program to print out a column of ten stars. She had coded:

```
10 X = "*"
20 FOR X = 1 to 10
30 PRINT X
40 NEXT X
```

Here the student had used one variable for two roles and had employed a variable type restricted to numeric data mistakenly for a character string. When she ran the program, she received the error message, "Type mismatch in 10." She asked the experimenter what a type mismatch was and the experimenter directed her to line 10, asking, "What kind of a symbol is the star, a number or a character?" Brenda answered, "A number, no a character." The experimenter then responded with, "Okay, and what is X? What does it stand for?" Brenda answered, "Oh, a number," and proceeded to recode the line, retrieving on her own the "$" needed to convert a numeric variable type to a character type. So the experimenter's hints led the student to recover knowledge that she possessed but had not accessed.

Behaviors such as those described in the examples above, as well as instances where students used knowledge in garbled ways but could sort things out with a little prompting, led us to characterize many student difficulties not as problems of missing knowledge but of "fragile knowledge," including inert knowledge, as illustrated above. Inert knowledge designates knowledge present but not accessed in problem-solving situations.

PROBLEMS OF ACCESS IN OTHER DOMAINS

Beyond the boundaries of programming, evidence is accumulating that people often know far more than they manage to bring to bear in problem-solving situations. In the field of expository writing, Bereiter and Scardamalia (1982, 1985) have found that children commonly are much better informed about a topic than their writing might first suggest. In studies with children in the elementary grades, these investigators found that many students, having stopped writing after producing an essay of less than 100 words on a large topic, typically give the explanation that they can think of nothing more to say. Yet the authors note that it usually takes very little prompting to reveal much more potentially usable knowledge.

In addition, Bereiter and Scardamalia have discovered that children often have difficulty even naming topics about which they know quite a bit and topics about which, in contrast, they know very little (Scardamalia, Bereiter, & Woodruff, 1980). It is as though children do not know what they know. The authors suggest that this difficulty indicates a failure to survey memory effectively. They assert that the ability to inventory one's knowledge resources constitutes an important component of one's strategic repertoire.

Bransford and colleagues argue that the problem of knowing something and failing to use it when relevant is ubiquitous (Bransford, Franks, Vye, & Sherwood, 1989). For example, they cite research in which college students were taught a problem-solving strategy based on five steps, with the acronym IDEAL (Bransford & Stein, 1984). Students found the material easy to learn and could paraphrase the model as well as identify examples of its usefulness. Nevertheless, there were many instances in which students could have profited from the model yet failed to do so. As an example, the authors noted that, unless explicitly prompted to do so, students often failed to realize how the model's counsel on problem identification and definition related to attempts to formulate the topic of a paper.

As a further example, Bransford et al. (1989) describe a circumstance reported by Bereiter (1984) in which a teacher of educational psychology gave her students a difficult article to read and told them they had ten minutes to learn as much as they could about it. Although all of the students had taken reading courses which taught them to skim for main ideas, consult section headings, and so on, nearly every student began with the first sentence of the article and then read straight through the article until the time was up.

In an investigation of adolescents' and adults' informal reasoning, Perkins and colleagues discovered that people substantially underutilize their knowledge base in attempting to reason about everyday issues (Perkins, in press; Perkins, Bushey, & Farady, in press). Pressed to think carefully and develop full considerations on both sides of an issue, people soon reported that they were "running dry." However, minimal prompting that was not specific to the issue at hand generally provoked subjects to provide several more reasons on both sides of the case. Not unsurprisingly, subjects tended to neglect the other side of the case — the side opposite their own. Under prompting conditions, subjects increased their yield of "other side" reasons an average of 700% percent!

In general then, problems of inert domain knowledge and knowledge fragile in other ways as well appear to trouble human problem solving in diverse contexts. Whether and how problem solvers can learn to access such knowledge better becomes a crucial issue in understanding the potentials of students to develop better problem-solving skills.

"POP UP" AND "DIG OUT" ACCESS TO LOCAL KNOWLEDGE

These concerns about the accessibility of fragile knowledge relate intimately to the questions raised at the outset about the role of general knowledge in problem solving. Indeed, the same studies that document the shortfall in the use of specific knowledge also point to the likely importance of such general knowledge in providing strategic prompts.

In particular, in clinical interviews we found that students in need of help were often responsive to higher level strategic prompts. In fact, about one third of the time such prompts enabled students to move forward and resolve the programming difficulty at hand (Perkins & Martin, 1986; Perkins, Martin, & Farady, 1986). For yet another specific example, in the square of stars problem described above, students commonly indicated a need to repeat a row of stars the desired number of times, but couldn't seem to continue from there. The prompt, "Do you know a command for repeating?" was often enough to get the student back on track.

Particularly notable was the range of the prompts that proved serviceable. Some sample prompts, selected for their variety, include: "How would you describe the problem to yourself?", "What do you need to do next?", "What does a semicolon do?" (when the student was reading a statement with a semicolon), "What's the first thing you need to tell the computer to do?", "Do you know a command that does this sort of thing?" (after the student has indicated a specific need, for example a need to repeat something), and "Are there any other ways to make the computer do X?" (e.g., print across, repeat something). While some prompts were phrased much more specifically than others, they in fact linked a very general question to particular circumstances. For example, "What does the semicolon do?" is a special case of "What does *this* do?" where *this* might be a symbol in any domain, from an algebraic expression to a part of a carburetor.

We recognize, of course, that whether a prompt succeeds depends not only on the prompt itself, but also on the organization and accessibility of the knowledge the prompt is intended to activate. Thus, the same prompt can succeed with one student and fail with another. For example, when asked, "Do you know a command for repeating something?" one student replied, "Oh, yeah. FOR-NEXT." However, another student replied, "GOTO." Sometimes a strategic prompt is just not enough to enable the student to get back on track. Nonetheless, our findings are suggestive of the importance of attending to generalized knowledge embodied in prompts in the pursuit of successful retrieval of domain-specific knowledge.

Of particular interest is the fact that for the most part such prompts apparently do not reflect any special knowledge the experimenter might have of the particular difficulty of the student. Consider once again the example cited earlier of the student solving the square of stars problem who achieved a row of 25 stars but was unable to continue from there. The general prompt given by the experimenter, "What do you need to do?" reflects no privileged insight into the specific nature of the programming problem. In general, the experimenters prompted with questions that students might well have asked themselves.

In summary then, these results suggest that the appropriate use of local knowledge may depend in part on self-cueing in the learner, the cues having a much more general character than the knowledge they help to retrieve.

At the same time, it must be recognized that other mechanisms also can contribute to the active use of knowledge. For example, Bransford and his colleagues (Bransford et al., 1989; Sherwood, Kinzer, Bransford, & Franks, 1987) have shown that learning in an active context of application considerably enhances the later availability of knowledge for other similar applications. To be sure, this knowledge access apparent in the active problem-solving context might be the result of student acquisition of some self-cueing practices which they carried over to new contexts. However, we think it more likely in interventions of this sort that some of the knowledge becomes partly "compiled" into productions with conditions sensitive to various patterns of possible application. On later occasions, these productions "trigger" the necessary information, accounting for the more active use.

We see this access path as distinct from the active use of self-cueing. We suggest that the two are complementary. A useful metaphor for the distinction refers to "pop up" versus "dig out" access. "Pop up" access occurs when a compiled production triggers, proposing the knowledge structure to be applied. "Pop up" access is likely to reflect local knowledge closely tied to particular contextual conditions for activation. In contrast, "dig out" access occurs when the individual engages in a self-cueing process that finds its way to the knowledge structure in question (cf. Perkins & Salomon, 1987; Salomon & Perkins, 1984, 1987). Because "dig out" access originates in cueing by self (or others) that reflects general knowledge of the sorts of questions that might be asked, in principle "dig out" access can retrieve knowledge further afield from the immediate associates of the context.

The work of Bransford and his colleagues suggests the importance of "pop up" access, while the cueing work with young programmers discussed above argues for the importance of "dig out" access. Of course, the two processes complement one another. There is no need to choose between them since both seem likely to be important mechanisms for putting more knowledge into active and appropriate use.

GENERAL AND LOCAL KNOWLEDGE IN DESIGNING A "METACOURSE" TO ENHANCE PROGRAMMING PERFOMANCE

Unlike many contexts of school learning, programming instruction routinely presents new concepts — for instance, new commands — in a context of use. This ought to provide for some degree of "pop up" access. But access is not as prevalent as one would like, as our research has shown. Accordingly, it is natural in the context of programming to seek to foster both "pop up" and "dig out" access in attempting to help students to make better use of their knowledge.

With this and some other concerns about elementary programming instruction in mind, over the past several years our team has developed and tested a "meta-course" to enhance students' mastery of elementary BASIC programming at the secondary school level (Perkins, Schwartz, & Simmons, 1988; Schwartz, Niguidula, & Perkins, 1988). By definition, a metacourse is designed to provide students with an empowering metacognitive layer of strategies and mental models relevant to a domain. A metacourse does not displace the subject matter as conventionally taught, but supplements it with strategies and mental models. Consequently, the metacourse requires only a modest percentage of the total instructional time. Evaluation of this intervention has yielded positive results, which will be discussed in the next section. First, let us focus on some of the issues of design, where, to bring general heuristics into contact with the particulars of the subject matter, it often seems appropriate to contextualize general ideas somewhat to suit the vocabulary and conceptual structure of a discipline.

One case in point is a mental model of the computer that figures centrally in the BASIC metacourse. The computer is represented to the students, both in posters and in an animated display, as a "Data Factory" with a robot named NAB (for "Not Awfully Bright") that is extremely limited in the actions it can perform within that environment. Further, there are only a few distinct areas within the data factory, such as the "program area," the "variables area," the "user input area," and so on. NAB runs around picking up commands from the program area, fetching values from the variables area, and in general carrying out the business of executing a program. NAB's actions are imagined and discussed with the help of the poster and are actually animated in the animated display. After NAB is introduced, the students are encouraged to make "mental movies" of what NAB does in the data factory as they write programs or when they are trying to debug programs in order to understand what the computer is doing.

The rationale for the data factory with NAB is straightforward: Students often prove unable to hand-execute programs, even though (according to the clinical research above) they often have considerable information about what commands do. It seems as though students need a mental organizer to help them consolidate that knowledge and to allow them to envision the computer's behavior. The data factory image is an effort to provide such an organizer, with "not awfully bright" NAB functioning as an explicit way of saying that the computer does not understand the programmer's intentions. This odd name has as its target another common shortfall in novice programmers: the belief that the computer in some sense knows what they are trying to do and will actively abet the process (DuBoulay, 1986; Pea, 1986).

The idea of modeling and imaging has been shown to be useful in a variety of academic and ill-defined problem situations (Gentner & Stevens, 1983; Johnson-Laird, 1983). Mayer (1976, 1981) has demonstrated the efficacy of a mental model for the computer in short-term teaching experiments where students studied a simplified computer language. Despite this evidence for the utility of mental models, the treatment of modeling and imaging in the BASIC metacourse does not stress the idea of modeling in general. Rather, the emphasis is on how the specific data factory model can prove useful for learning BASIC. In some additional materials now being developed for the metacourse, we do encourage students to consider the general utility of modeling because we believe that this will enrich their understanding of the data factory model and may spill over to other contexts as well. Nonetheless, the specific data factory model remains the focus.

Why? Well, one alternative would be to introduce the general idea of modeling and guide students in evolving their own models of the computer. But, in our view, asking beginners to evolve their own models of the computer is likely to be too much of a challenge, one that novices are not apt to achieve well or quickly. Thus the BASIC metacourse highlights a "pre-contextualized" model rather than the general idea of modeling. We recognize that other developers might want to explore a different balance, but that debate need not be engaged here. The key point for the present argument is that there *is* a balance to strike, with tradeoffs to be considered, when one brings general knowledge to bear on problems of local knowledge.

The same issue arises in another central BASIC metacourse strategy: All commands are discussed in terms of a trio of organizing concepts: *purpose, syntax,* and *action.* Students are encouraged to think about the purpose of a command, examine its exact syntax, and envision its precise action in the data factory as executed by NAB. *Purpose* directly addresses the common novice problem, documented in our clinical work, of failing to associate commands with their typical functions within programs. *Syntax* directly reminds students to pay attention to this generally troublesome area. *Action* is yet another reminder to use the data factory model, with an emphasis on understanding just exactly what the command in question asks NAB to do.

The *purpose, syntax, action* trio actually derived from some concepts of more general utility. One source for the trio was three questions associated with a cross-disciplinary scheme for fostering thinking in the subject matters called *knowledge as design* (Perkins, 1986a,b). In *knowledge as design*, students are encouraged to inquire about the purpose, structure, model cases, and arguments of things and concepts. In the *purpose, syntax, action* trio, the term purpose was inherited directly, while syntax and action are aspects of structure and model. Another source contributing to the same trio was the contrasts among syntax, semantics, and pragmatics. Syntax was inherited directly, while semantics corresponds to action and pragmatics to purpose.

The tradeoff alluded to before in considering models is plain. Because the quartet of concepts from knowledge as design and the *syntax, semantics, pragmatics* trio are less domain-specific, they require more interpretation in the context of programming to yield their benefits. The *purpose, syntax, action* trio, with its narrower focus, is more easily applied to programming and thus in the design of the present metacourse is preferred over the more general taxonomies. Again the emphasis is on the utility of novice's self-cueing—posing questions about the purpose, structure, and syntax of commands in the learning of BASIC—rather than pointing out that these are but a special case of more encompassing methods of general analysis applicable to a great variety of problems.

Still another example of this contextualizing of general metacognitive strategies to fit more closely the structure of BASIC programming is manifested in the metacourse treatment of debugging. Many of the metacognitive strategies used to locate, diagnose, and fix bugs in programs are also helpful when unforeseen outcomes occur in other complex systems or processes — everything from medical diagnosis and automobile troubleshooting to problems with a recipe, a political campaign, or a personal relationship. However, the metacourse materials make little mention of these other contexts.

For example, the procedure used in locating one's lost keys by recalling where you definitely know you had them last and where you realized you did not have them is analogous to the strategy in debugging programs where you consider that part of the program between the point where you are certain the program is functioning well and where it is clearly not doing so. Likewise, such general heuristics as "working backwards," "means-ends analysis," and generating "flow of control" diagrams are utilized in physics, engineering, mathematics, logic, and other domains as well as in programming when debugging or, more generally, error detection strategies are required.

However, rather than emphasize these heuristics in their general form, the metacourse focuses on concrete contextualizations such as attending to error messages, inserting "PRINT" statements, and inputting "real data." Some new materials we are developing do draw students' attention to generic debugging principles. Nonetheless, the weight falls on formulations designed to function well in the programming context specifically because it can be difficult for students to bridge the gap between very general formulations and domain-specific applications.

In summary, design dilemmas encountered in the metacourse demonstrate how powerful heuristic ideas often can be formulated at different levels of generality — highly generalized versus contextualized — to facilitate particular disciplinary applications. Tradeoffs between the effectiveness of more general and local versions have to be confronted in any context of instructional design when one wishes to foster self-cueing as a means of accessing local knowledge.

THE IMPACT OF A METACOURSE FOR PROGRAMMING

The various considerations discussed above certainly seem relevant to the design of an effective metacognitive supplement for programming. Of course, the bottom-line question remains: Does it work? Although the main business of this chapter is not to recount the details of evaluating the programming metacourse, a brief account of our efforts to evaluate its impact is appropriate.

We designed our evaluation of the metacourse with three main questions in mind: Did the metacourse prove to be "teachable," leading to an implementation that smoothly introduced the intended concepts and encouraged their use? Did the metacourse have the hoped-for impact on students' mastery of BASIC programming? Finally, did the metacourse have an impact on more general cognitive skills, even though no special effort was made to highlight such skills? In order to gather evidence on these questions we employed a number of assessment procedures, including the development of a general cognitive skills test and a BASIC achievement test, along with a classroom observation rating sheet and student questionnaire.

The cognitive skills instrument was designed to test skill in formal syllogistic reasoning, complex linear reasoning, field-independence and planning, accuracy in describing a complex geometric figure, and two "near transfer" tasks: translating a deceptively simple word problem into an algebraic equation (a version of the well-known "students and professors" problem of Ehrlich, Soloway, & Abbott, 1982, and Soloway, Lochhead, & Clement, 1982) and describing some events using a restricted language containing the words "repeat" and "decide."

The BASIC test was a fairly standard paper and pencil programming test, formulated to evaluate certain general programming skills — the ability to hand-execute, debug, and break a problem into subtasks — as well as to test knowledge about programming commands typically presented in an introductory BASIC course (PRINT, LET, FOR/NEXT, IF-THEN, etc.).

A small formative study was conducted with an initial set of metacourse materials in the spring of 1986. The results, reported in Perkins, Farady, Simmons, and Villa (1986), indicated that the metacourse was eminently teachable, with no major problems of teacher preparation. However, the effects on BASIC performance, while encouraging, were inconclusive due to problems involving initial differences between experimental and control groups.

The results of a much larger study, conducted with 15 teachers and over 300 students at 13 high schools, were much clearer (Perkins et al., 1988). The experimental groups produced about 77% correct responses on the BASIC performance posttest compared to about 66% for the control groups ($p<.001$). Furthermore, the experimental groups did significantly better than the controls on all major categories of problems, with the smallest advantage occurring on simple one line command problems and production problems (a mean difference of about one third of a standard deviation) and the largest on the hand execution problems (nearly two thirds of one standard deviation). The gain in hand execution performance can be taken as evidence of the utility of mental modeling in helping students to organize and deploy their knowledge of BASIC.

As noted previously, the metacourse was designed specifically to advance programming skills rather than to promote general transfer. Nonetheless, the data on the cognitive skills pretest-posttest gain scores provided an opportunity to explore the issue within this limited context. Some evidence of transfer was observed in the experimental groups, but only on the problem most closely related to that of producing coherent commands in a programming language, the "Repeats and Decides" subtest. No such advantage was found for performance on the "students and professors" problem, despite prior suggestions in the literature that programming experience might help with students' understanding of such problems (Ehrlich et al., 1982; Soloway et al., 1982).

A follow-up test on a small sample of these students who were enrolled in a year-long BASIC course indicated the persistence of the gains in BASIC performance five months later. A more recent study with a different group of students and teachers produced no transfer effects outside of programming at all, but yielded nearly identical improvements on BASIC performance, thus making it unlikely that experimental group gains were due to some advantageous distribution of teachers (Schwartz, Perkins, Estey, Kruidenier, & Simmons, 1987).

Thus, the metacourse constructed for elementary BASIC has demonstrably enhanced students' programming performance, improving performance by about one half of one standard deviation in comparison with control groups. Note that the metacourse supplementation teaches no new content, for instance, particular commands. Accordingly, these findings lend credence to the idea that provision of resources for self-cueing and mental modeling can enhance "dig out" and "pop up" access.

GENERAL AND LOCAL KNOWLEDGE IN TEACHING FOR TRANSFER FROM PROGRAMMING

The themes of "dig out" and "pop up" access and of general knowledge contextualized to particular domains relate intimately to what has become a controversial issue in some psychological and educational circles, namely, the potential of programming to foster the development of cognitive skills transferrable to other contexts. A number of authors have argued that programming seems in many ways an especially fertile seedbed of cognitive skills—encouraging and exercising mental organization and precise thinking, seeing the world in terms of procedures, and fostering other patterns of cognition (see Feurzeig, Horwitz, & Nickerson, 1981; Linn, 1985; Papert, 1980).

At the same time, the literature on expertise and the local knowledge findings alluded to earlier suggest that there is no particular reason to expect instruction in programming to yield transferrable skills. If local knowledge dominates in problem solving, by definition such local knowledge ought not to be very relevant to other contexts. Moreover, the process of developing expertise in a domain is said to operate contrary to generalization—since general knowledge supposedly becomes compiled into productions fine-tuned to the particular context (Anderson, 1983).

What then does the empirical track record show about the impact of programming on general cognitive skills? And what do the results of such research suggest about the relationship between general and particular knowledge in problem solving?

On the whole, the findings have been in keeping with the preeminence of the local knowledge position. In a number of studies that have used a diversity of instruments to examine general cognitive payoffs from programming, negative results have emerged (e.g., Blume, 1984; Clements, 1985b; Dalbey & Linn, 1985; Kurland, Clement, Mawby, & Pea, 1986; Kurland, Pea, Clement, & Mawby, 1987; Land & Turner, 1985; Pea & Kurland, 1984a, 1984b). However, in a few cases positive results have been obtained. For example, Clements and his colleagues have conducted several experiments where young students of Logo were encouraged to think actively about what they were doing as they did it, in a quasi-clinical setting (Clements, 1985a; Clements & Gullo, 1984; Clements & Merriman, in press). These students showed marked gains on a variety of cognitive instruments. Carver and Klahr (1987) also designed an intervention highlighting debugging skills and stressing the potentials of transfer. Transfer was again observed.

These findings are inconsistent with the strong local knowledge position that performance in one domain does not transfer to other domains. But the findings leave a puzzle: how to account for the usually negative but occasionally positive findings? Some help with this matter comes from a model of transfer proposed by Gavriel Salomon and David Perkins (Perkins & Salomon, 1987; Salomon & Perkins, 1984; Salomon & Perkins, 1987). These authors distinguish between two very different mechanisms of transfer called "low road transfer" and "high road transfer."

Low road transfer occurs when knowledge structures learned to near automaticity in one context are triggered in another because of perceptual resemblance. For example, people familiar with car driving find that they can easily drive small trucks, simply because the perceptual surround of a truck cab is enough like a car that it triggers a person's car-driving habits, and those habits fit the context of a truck well enough to be functional. When the old knowledge does not fit the new context, the results can be ineffectual or even negative. For example, right-side driving habits acquired in the United States can yield dangerous low road transfer when an American tourist rents a car in England. Also, regardless of how relevant in principle the old knowledge, when the new perceptual surround does not evoke the old knowledge, it does no good. For instance, Gentner (1987) reports an experiment in which subjects could easily elaborate relevant analogies once the analogies were pointed out but generally did not discover the analogies on their own because of differences in the surface characteristics of the contexts.

While low road transfer depends on automatized knowledge structures and automatic triggering, high road transfer does not. High road transfer occurs when a person mindfully abstracts knowledge structures from one situation and carries them across to another. For example, an amateur chess player entering local politics might generalize and apply the well-known chess principle, "seek control of the center," by pondering what "center" might mean in the political context — center of opinion, communication, political leverage, and so on — and making plans to exercise control at such loci. Similarly, a person might generalize a strategic reading plan learned in a special reading course, such as "stop before you start reading and think what you're going to do," to a more overarching impulse control plan: "No matter what you're about to do, stop before you start and think what you're going to do."

In summary, in high road transfer mindful attention and active processing to abstract and contextualize knowledge structures takes the place of the spontaneous triggering of automatized structures characteristic of low road transfer. The connection between old knowledge and new application is made in quite a different way.

The low road - high road model helps to explain the inconsistent results from research on the general cognitive impact of learning to program. First of all, the typical failure to find signs of transfer is consistent with the predictions of the low road – high road model because in most programming instruction neither the conditions for low road transfer nor those for high road transfer are met. Regarding low road transfer, novice programmers typically do not master much of anything to near automaticity. Nor do the sorts of transfer applications usually probed bear any surface resemblance to contexts of programming. Thus, low road transfer would not be expected. Regarding high road transfer, typical programming instruction does little to provoke students to think metacognitively about their problem solving or learning processes in programming or to reflect upon the possible applications outside of programming. In other words, there is no explicit emphasis on the mindful abstraction characteristic of high road transfer.

The few examples of positive transfer from programming to problems of quite different sorts also can be understood in terms of the low road - high road model. These cases of transfer all have involved circumstances in which learners were encouraged to reflect upon their programming activities and abstract salient characteristics. In other words, the positive findings have occurred in circumstances conducive to high road transfer.

How does all this relate to the present themes of knowledge access, "pop up" and "dig out" access, and the role of more general knowledge in deploying local knowledge? Basically, low road transfer is a "pop up" process of knowledge access and high road transfer is a "dig out" process. The negative findings from research efforts to transfer general skills learned in programming to other contexts indicate that "pop up" access is not likely to reach very far. Nor is "dig out" access likely to occur unless the person is in circumstances where he deploys general knowledge to stir up particular knowledge that might apply elsewhere and carry it over.

For example, in "digging out" principles for high road transfer, a person might ask him- or herself questions like these: "Well, what do I know that might fit here? I've played a lot of chess. This isn't chess, but maybe there are some connections. Can I see any? What about some other area where I have plenty of experience?" And so on. Such self-cues constitute very general strategic knowledge about how to provoke one's thinking processes. Their effects are played out upon the more local knowledge that the cues stir up. In summary, the pattern of findings in the research on transfer from programming, which might at first be taken to support a pure local knowledge position, in fact is consistent with the more complex position argued here, where local knowledge and general knowledge function together in a kind of synergy in nonroutine contexts.

HOW GENERAL AND PARTICULAR MEET:
A FRACTAL CONCEPT OF MIND

Examining problem solving in programming, we have discussed clinical research, instructional design decisions, and results of teaching experiments that call into question an extreme local knowledge position about the nature of effective problem solving. According to our results, students often do not have access to the local knowledge that in some sense they possess. General cueing can help to provide access. There are design dilemmas about the most helpful level of generality for self-cues and mental models, with recognition that ideas may prove useful at more than one level of generality.

Research focused on other disciplines also argues for the importance of taking into account the interplay between general and local knowledge in effective problem solving. For example, Alan Schoenfeld's successful experiments in teaching mathematical problem solving have emphasized some specifically mathematical heuristics, such as mathematical induction, some more general heuristics, such as the use of diagramming, and some extremely general problem management strategies, such as reviewing one's progress periodically and assessing whether the current approach is serving well (Schoenfeld, 1979a, 1979b, 1980, 1982, 1985; Schoenfeld & Herrmann, 1982). John Clement's studies of persons well-acquainted with physics addressing nonstandard problems offers evidence of the involvement of knowledge at many levels of generality (Clement, 1982, in press).

In light of these challenges to an extreme local knowledge position, how should we conceptualize the role of general and local knowledge in problem solving? Sometimes it is useful to dramatize an interpretation with an evocative image. In this case, we suggest the image of a fractal. Many will be familiar with the idea of fractals because of their current popularity in discussions relating mathematics to natural phenomena. Fractals are geometric structures that repeat the same forms at many levels of scale. Thus for example, a fractal might consist of a large Z-shaped form, the segments of which are made of smaller Z-shaped forms, the segments of which are made of yet smaller Z-shaped forms, and so on down to as fine a grain as desired.

In constructing the analogy between fractal structures and thought processes, we identify scale with generality. Just as a fractal involves certain forms that occur at many levels of scale, so thought in challenging circumstances involves concepts that occur at various levels of generality, in various degrees of contextualization. Just as this multi-level character of fractals imparts to them their peculiarly rich texture, we suggest that it is the involvement of the same concepts at multiple levels of contextualization that makes thinking about challenging problems rich and compelling.

Of course, this fractal metaphor for mental organization in problem solving cannot be extended very far. We see it as no more than an anchoring image for a more careful account of the interplay between knowledge of various levels of generality in problem solving. Nevertheless, several aspects of the analogy shed light on this interplay.

How Fractal Families Occur

How does it come about that a particular concept forms a "fractal family," with

AUGUSTANA UNIVERSITY COLLEGE
LIBRARY

more and less contextualized versions of the concept occurring in the same problem-solving activity? Actually, a number of different scenarios seem relevant.

Constructing contextualizations on the spot. Sometimes a general concept leads to a contextualized interpretation constructed during the problem-solving process. For instance, suppose that a computer programmer working on a complex program asks himself, "What now?" This is a general self-cue to seek a purpose. It leads to the programmer recognizing the need to test for a certain condition. So far, the matter has nothing to do with programming specifically, just with the logic of the matter at hand. The programmer then figures out that to carry out this test, one must check for the presence of a certain substring within a character string. Not having confronted the problem before, the programmer constructs a search routine that does the job.

The programmer's thinking thus encompasses several members of a fractal family: the original general probe for an immediate purpose contextualized to the need to test, contextualized to a particular kind of test, contextualized further to a particular means-end structure, the search routine itself. The first version is fully general, applicable to any context. The second is specific to the context of the overall task but not to the enterprise of programming. The third engages the data structures of the programming approach. The fourth addresses a particular programming solution.

Cueing prior contextualizations. Now suppose this programmer in the future is developing a somewhat analogous program. The programmer again asks, "What now?" Recognizing familiar circumstances, the programmer cues up the need to test, reconstructing the details as necessary. That achievement in turn serves to cue up the particular kind of test, again with reconstruction of details as necessary. There follows the cueing up of the particular search routine needed to effect the test. In other words, the already established fractal family is reactivated in a top-down manner, a process of "dig out" access.

Triggering established contextualizations. With extended experience on the sort of problem in question, the programmer might evolve a direct recognitional link between the circumstances and the search routine. The programmer does not have to ask himself, "What now?" or even to think about any of the intermediate steps indicated. The programmer simply recognizes the situation as calling for the search routine and installs it. The top-down "dig out" process has been short-circuited by "pop up" knowledge that simply pops into place on the appropriate occasion. To put it another way, the original top-down process has become compiled into a production that directly triggers installation of the search routine under rather specific conditions.

This does not mean, however, that a fractal family is not involved. For one thing, it *was* involved historically in the evolution of the "pop up" knowledge. Moreover, suppose the programmer encounters circumstances where the subroutine is relevant but the circumstances have some novelty and do not match the pattern that triggers the "pop up" knowledge. Then the full fractal family is likely to come into play again, and all the more easily because of prior experience.

Partial use of a family. Of course, facing various programming situations, a programmer may find the contextualization sequence useful up to a point, with the need then to cut in a new direction to resolve contextual variations. Perhaps, for instance, the programmer has to test for characters embedded in a string, but this time they may not be contiguous. The old search routine will not do. The programmer needs to construct a new contextualization of the general plan to accommodate to the variant situation.

Abstraction rather than contextualization. We have emphasized situations in which a programmer might construct a fractal family of concepts from the top down. But, of course, programmers and problem solvers of all sorts also make generalizations, provoked for example by opportunities for analogizing between one programming situation and another to solve a problem in the second. In such circumstances, one may construct a fractal family bottom-up, generalizing previously established elements of knowledge. Again, both the original knowledge and the more general representations have their utility

The Role of Local Knowledge

The foregoing remarks have sought to make plausible the importance of relatively general knowledge in problem solving. But what about the evidence for the importance of local knowledge?

One answer already discussed is that local knowledge plays a dominant role in expert handling of problems typical of the domain. This is the case identified above as "triggering established contextualizations." However, the role of local knowledge is much more extensive than that. Local knowledge figures constantly in the use of more general knowledge in that local knowledge mediates the process of contextualization.

To return to the example developed earlier, suppose a programmer prompts him- or herself with a "What now?" question. This very general cue can hardly lead to anything relevant to the program under development without provoking access to the programmer's very specific representations of the project underway. Those representations give the general question a context. Likewise, after the programmer has recognized that a test for a certain condition is necessary, further contextualization requires local knowledge about how that condition might be manifested in the data structures employed in the program.

General knowledge, then, is useless in particular cases unless contextualized, and local knowledge always must figure crucially in contextualization. Accordingly, in keeping with the stance of those involved in the research on expertise, local knowledge plays an absolutely crucial role *even* in problems not so typical of the domain. Local knowledge is critical in such problems because the problem solver will need considerable local knowledge to contextualize general knowledge to the needs of the atypical problem.

However, notice that in atypical problems in a domain, local knowledge provides a necessary, but not a sufficient condition, to a successful solution. Exactly because the problem solver's local knowledge was developed on problems more typical of the domain, the local knowledge by itself is not likely to permit dealing with novel problems. That is, there will be nothing close to a ready made solution path that can "pop up" and resolve a novel problem. Rather, the person's local knowledge of the domain has application in more roundabout ways; the roundabout ways needs to be "dug out" through the use of more general knowledge.

Reassessing the Power-Generality Tradeoff

Very general problem-solving methods often are referred to as "weak methods," as noted earlier, with reference to a "power-generality tradeoff." The idea is that general methods provide much less leverage in problem-solving situations than local knowledge. When we begin work in a domain, general methods are all we have to work with. We don't do very well, but we do the best we can. As we discover things about the particulars of the domain, our general methods become contextualized into "pop up" knowledge that is fine-tuned to the needs of the domain and also become part of our local knowledge about the domain. We have left the generality behind and won the power of particularized knowledge structures.

What does the fractal view of problem solving say in response to this picture? Basically, we would like to argue that to speak of general methods as weak is to make an overgeneralization. Rather, one should ask, "*When* are general methods weak and in what ways?"

General methods certainly are weak when one lacks local knowledge to contextualize their application. Then one must work hard to build appropriate contextualizations and may well fail. General methods certainly are weak when no attention is given to the process of contextualization, even supposing considerable local knowledge. For instance, suppose one teaches problem-solving heuristics and problem management techniques to students who have a fairly good knowledge of programming or mathematics but plenty of room to improve their problem solving. These problem-solving heuristics and problem management techniques will not help unless the students manage to bring them into contact with local knowledge. Without some attention in the instruction to the appropriate contextualization of the general methods instructing students in the "dig out" enterprise, the general methods are not likely to pay off.

But general methods can be strong. They can show their strength when there is a local knowledge base to mediate the contextualizing that must occur in each application *and* when the contextualizing process itself has received some attention. In such circumstances, general methods provide higher-order control structures that can substantially increase the utility of the local knowledge one has available. Without those control structures, the local knowledge only functions by "popping up." With these control structures mediating "dig out" access, local knowledge can be brought to bear much more flexibly upon problems within the domain, and perhaps sometimes beyond the domain.

To summarize, in the fractal picture of mind we are painting, general and local knowledge exist in a symbiotic relationship. Local knowledge does not displace general knowledge as mastery develops. Rather, local knowledge develops through the compilation of general knowledge, but general knowledge continues to serve important control functions that, through "dig out" access, deploy local knowledge much more widely than "pop up" access would allow. This fractal character in problem solving becomes particularly salient and important when novel problems are encountered.

This perspective also has implications for instructional practice. It warns against an exclusive emphasis on local knowledge and on the presumption that local knowledge will automatically prove operative. It recommends attention to multiple levels of generality and to the processes of contextualization and abstraction that mediate between them.

Respecting the literature on expertise, one can acknowledge that general knowledge is helpless without local knowledge. But one must also recognize that local knowledge is rigid without general knowledge. Then what sort of knowledge is powerful? Really, it is the team that is powerful, the fractal structure with concepts occurring in variations at multiple levels of generality. Although developing these ideas in the context of programming, we suggest that this fractal picture of the role of generality in problem solving applies equally well to most other domains (cf. Perkins & Salomon, 1989).

Acknowledgements

The research reported here was conducted at the Educational Technology Center of the Harvard Graduate School of Education, operating with suport from the Office of Educational Research and Improvement (contract #OERI 400-83-0041). Opinions expressed herein are not necessarily shared by OERI and do not represent Office policy.

REFERENCES

Anderson, J. R. (1983). *The architecture of cognition.* Cambridge, MA: Harvard University Press.

Bereiter, C. (1984). How to keep thinking skills from going the way of all frills. *Educational Leadership, 42,* 75-77.

Bereiter, C., & Scardamalia, M. (1982). From conversation to composition: The role of instruction in a developmental process. In R. Glaser (Ed.), *Advances in instructional psychology* (Vol. 2, pp. 1-64). Hillsdale, NJ: Lawrence Erlbaum Associates.

64 PERKINS, SCHWARTZ, SIMMONS

Bereiter, C., & Scardamalia, M. (1985). Cognitive coping strategies and the problem of inert knowledge. In S. S. Chipman, J. W. Segal, & R. Glazer (Eds.), *Thinking and learning skills: Current research and open questions* (pp. 65-80). Hillsdale, NJ: Lawrence Erlbaum Associates.

Blume, B. W. (1984, April). *A review of research on the effects of computer programming on mathematical problem solving.* Paper presented at the annual meeting of the American Educational Research Association, New Orleans, LA.

Bransford, J. D., Franks, J. J., Vye, N. J., & Sherwood, R. D. (1989). *New approaches to instruction: Because wisdom can't be told.* In S. Vosniadou & A. Ortony (Eds.) *Similarity and analogical reasoning.* (pp. 470-497). NY: Cambridge University Press.

Bransford, J., & Stein, B. (1984). *The IDEAL problem solver.* New York: Freeman.

Carver, S. M., & Klahr, D. (April, 1987). *Analysis, instruction, and transfer of the components of debugging skill.* Paper presented at the Biennial meeting of the Society for Research in Child Development, Baltimore, MD.

Chase, W. C., & Simon, H. A. (1973). Perception in chess. *Cognitive Psychology, 4,* 55-81.

Chi, M. T. H., Glaser, R., & Rees, E. (1982). Expertise in problem solving. In R. Sternberg (Ed.), *Advances in the psychology of human intelligence* (pp. 7-75). Hillsdale, NJ: Lawrence Erlbaum Associates.

Clement, J. (1982, August). *Analogical reasoning patterns in expert problem solving.* Paper presented at the Fourth Annual Conference of the Cognitive Science Society. Ann Arbor, MI.

Clement, J. (in press). Nonformal reasoning in physics: The use of analogies and extreme cases. In J. Voss, D. N. Perkins, & J. Segal (Eds.), *Informal reasoning.* Hillsdale, NJ: Lawrence Erlbaum Associates.

Clements, D. H. (1985a, April). *Effects of Logo programming on cognition, metacognitive skills, and achievement.* Presentation at the meeting of the American Educational Research Association, Chicago, IL.

Clements, D. H. (1985b). Research on Logo in education: Is the turtle slow but steady, or not even in the race? *Computers in the Schools, 2* (2/3), 55-71.

Clements, D. H., & Gullo, D. F. (1984). Effects of computer programming on young children's cognition. *Journal of Educational Psychology, 76*(6), 1051-1058.

Clements, D. H., & Merriman, S. (in press). Componential developments in Logo programming environments. In R. Mayer (Ed.), *Teaching and learning computer programming: Multiple research perspectives.* Hillsdale, NJ: Lawrence Erlbaum Associates.

Dalbey, J., & Linn, M. C. (1985). The demands and requirements of computer programming: A literature review. *Journal of Educational Computing Research, 1,* 253-274.

DuBoulay, B. (1986). Some difficulties of learning to program. *Journal of Educational Computing Research, 2* (1), 57-73.

Ehrlich, K., Soloway, E., & Abbott, V. (1982). *Transfer effects from programming to algebra word problems: A preliminary study* (Report No. 257). New Haven, CT: Yale University, Department of Computer Science.

Feurzeig, W., Horwitz, P., & Nickerson, R. (1981). *Microcomputers in education* (Report No. 4798). Cambridge, MA: Bolt, Beranek, & Newman.

Gentner, D. (1987). *Mechanisms of analogical learning.* Urbana, IL: University of Illinois, Department of Computer Science.

Gentner, D., & Stevens, A. L. (Eds.). (1983). *Mental models*. Hillsdale, NJ: Lawrence Erlbaum Associates.

Glaser, R. (1984). Education and thinking: The role of knowledge. *American Psychologist, 39* , 93-104.

Johnson-Laird, P. N. (1983). *Mental models*. Cambridge, MA: Harvard University Press.

Kurland, M. D., Clement, C., Mawby, R., & Pea, R. D. (1987). Mapping the cognitive demands of learning to program. In D. N. Perkins, J. Lochhead, & J. Bishop (Eds.), *Thinking: The second international conference* (pp. 333-358). Hillsdale, NJ: Lawrence Erlbaum Associates.

Kurland, D. M., Pea, R. D., Clement, C., & Mawby, R. (1986). *A study of the development of programming ability and thinking skills in high school students*. New York: Bank Street College of Education, Center for Children and Technology. Also, *Journal of Educational Computing Research,* in press.

Land, M. L., & Turner, S. V. (1985). *What are the effects of computer programming on cognitive skills?* Paper presented at the annual meeting of the Association for Educational Data Systems, Toronto, Ontario, Canada.

Larkin, J. H., McDermott, J., Simon, D. P., & Simon, H. A. (1980). Modes of competence in solving physics problems. *Cognitive Science, 4,* 317-345.

Linn, M. C. (1985). The cognitive consequences of programming instruction in classrooms. *Educational Researcher, 14,* 14-29.

Mayer, R. E. (1976). Some conditions of meaningful learning for computer programming: Advance organizers and subject control of frame order. *Journal of Educational Psychology, 68,* 143-150.

Mayer, R. E. (1981). The psychology of how novices learn computer programming. *Computing Surveys, 13* (11), 121-141.

Papert, S. (1980). *Mindstorms: Children, computers, and powerful ideas*. New York: Basic.

Pea, R. D. (1986). Language-independent conceptual "bugs" in novice programming. *Journal of Educational Computing Research ,* 2(1), 25-36.

Pea, R. D., & Kurland, D. M. (1984a). *Logo programming and the development of planning skills* (Report No. 16). New York: Bank Street College.

Pea, R. D., & Kurland, D. M. (1984b). On the cognitive effects of learning computer programming. *New Ideas in Psychology,* 2(2), 137-168.

Perkins, D. N. (1986a). *Knowledge as design*. Hillsdale, NJ: Lawrence Erlbaum Associates.

Perkins, D. N. (1986b). Knowledge as design: Teaching thinking through content. In J. B. Baron & R. S. Sternberg (Eds.), *Teaching thinking skills: Theory and practice* (pp. 62-85). New York: Freeman.

Perkins, D. N. (in press). Reasoning as it is and could be. In D. Topping, D. Crowell, & V. Kobayashi (Eds.), *Thinking: The third international conference*. Hillsdale, NJ: Lawrence Erlbaum Associates.

Perkins, D. N., Bushey, B. B., & Farady, M. (in press). Everyday reasoning and the roots of intelligence. In J. Voss, D. N. Perkins, & J. Segal (Eds.), *Informal reasoning*. Hillsdale, NJ: Lawrence Erlbaum Associates.

Perkins, D. N., Farady, M., Simmons, R., & Villa, E. (1986). *A "metacourse" to enhance the learning of BASIC*. (Tech. Rep. No. 86-12). Cambridge, MA, Harvard Graduate School of Education: Educational Technology Center.

Perkins, D. N., & Martin, F. (1986). Fragile knowledge and neglected strategies in novice programmers. In E. Soloway & S. Iyengar (Eds.), *Empirical studies of programmers* (pp. 213-219). Norwood, NJ: Ablex.

Perkins, D. N., Martin, F. & Farady, M. (1986). *Loci of difficulty in learning to program* (Technical Report No. 86-6). Cambridge, MA, Harvard Graduate School of Education: Educational Technology Center, .

Perkins, D., & Salomon, G. (1987). Transfer and teaching thinking. In D. N. Perkins, J. Lochhead, & J. Bishop (Eds.), *Thinking: The second international conference* (pp. 285-303). Hillsdale, NJ: Lawrence Erlbaum Associates.

Perkins, D. N., & Salomon, G. (1989). Are cognitive skills context-bound? *Educational Researcher, 18*(1), 16-25..

Perkins, D., Schwartz, S., & Simmons, R. (1988). Instructional strategies for the problems of novice programmers. In R. Mayer (Ed.), *Teaching and learning computer programming: Multiple research perspectives* (pp. 153- 178). Hillsdale, NJ: Lawrence Erlbaum Associates.

Salomon, G., & Perkins, D. N. (1984, August). *Rocky roads to transfer: Rethinking mechanisms of a neglected phenomenon.* Paper presented at the Conference on Thinking, Harvard Graduate School of Education, Cambridge, MA.

Salomon, G., & Perkins, D. N. (1987). Transfer of cognitive skills from programming: When and how? *Journal of Educational Computing Research, 3,* 149-169.

Scardamalia, M., Bereiter, C., & Woodruff, E. (1980). *The effects of content knowledge on writing.* Paper presented at the meeting of the American Educational Research Association, Boston, MA.

Schoenfeld, A. H. (1979a). Can heuristics be taught? In J. Lochhead & J. Clement (Eds.), *Cognitive process instruction* (pp. 315-338). Hillsdale, NJ: Lawrence Erlbaum Associates.

Schoenfeld, A. H. (1979b). Explicit heuristic training as a variable in problem solving performance. *Journal for Research in Mathematics Education, 10* (3), 173-187.

Schoenfeld, A. H. (1980). Teaching problem-solving skills. *American Mathematical Monthly, 87,* 794-805.

Schoenfeld, A. H. (1982). Measures of problem-solving performance and of problem-solving instruction. *Journal for Research in Mathematics Education, 13* (1), 31-49.

Schoenfeld, A. H. (1985). *Mathematical problem solving.* New York: Academic.

Schoenfeld, A. H., & Herrmann, D. J. (1982). Problem perception and knowledge structure in expert and novice mathematical problem solvers. *Journal of Experimental Psychology: Learning, Memory, and Cognition , 8,* 484-494.

Schwartz, S. H., Niguidula, D., & Perkins, D. N. (1988). A vitamin shot for BASIC classes. *The Computing Teacher, 15*(6), 62-64.

Schwartz, S. H., Perkins, D. N., Estey, G., Kruidenier, J., & Simmons, R. (1987). *An empirical study of a "Metacourse" to enhance the learning of BASIC* (ETC Technical Report #87-7). Cambridge, MA: Harvard Graduate School of Education, Educational Technology Center.

Sherwood, R. D., Kinzer, C. K., Bransford, J. D., & Franks, J. J. (1987). Some benefits of creating macro-contexts for science instruction: Initial findings. *Journal of Research in Science Teaching, 24,* 417-435.

Soloway, E., Lochhead, J., & Clement, J. (1982). Does computer programming enhance problem solving ability? Some positive evidence on algebra word problems. In R. Seidel, R. Anderson, & B. Hunter (Eds.), *Computer literacy* (pp. 171-185). New York: Academic.

5 A VIEW OF MATHEMATICAL PROBLEM SOLVING IN SCHOOL

James G. Greeno
Stanford University and the
Institute for Research on Learning

INTRODUCTION

The information-processing view of problem solving has achieved several major successes. Among them is the analysis of cognitive processes and knowledge structures involved in solving problems in school mathematics. This paper will begin with a brief review of results that have been obtained in these analyses, considering both the contributions to cognitive science that have been achieved, and some ways in which the resulting theoretical results are beginning to be used in educational practice. We now have clear theoretical pictures of the knowledge that text problems require, and these can be used to teach that problem-solving knowledge more effectively.

We can also use these clear theoretical pictures to ask whether the knowledge needed for text problems is what we want students to learn. In my view, the answer is that knowledge required for solving text problems is unacceptably limited. I will present this opinion and sketch an alternative view of mathematical knowing as an activity, rather than as a set of cognitive structures and processes. If we want students to become knowers of mathematics in this sense, the goals and methods of mathematical education need to be different from those of instructing them so they can solve text problems. I will describe some examples of classroom teaching that reflect these alternative goals and that also let us begin to see features of educational practice that could result in more valuable mathematical learning. Models of student thinking in textbook problem solving can play a useful role in this practice, but their use can be quite different from treating the models as cognitive objectives of instruction (e.g., Greeno, 1976).

Finally, I will discuss a set of research problems in mathematical cognition that we need to address in order to inform and support the reform of mathematics education. I will include some preliminary findings from a research project that I am conducting with several associates at Stanford, as an example of one kind of study that contributes to this agenda.

MODELS OF SOLVING TEXT PROBLEMS

Following Newell and Simon's (1972) watershed achievement in creating a new theoretical and empirical methodology for the psychology of problem solving, several researchers began using that methodology in the study of problem solving in mathematics. The idea was to examine students' performance as they work on problems, asking them to think aloud as they work, and to develop information-processing models that simulate the students' problem-solving activity. Formulated as computer programs, the models are tested by comparing the steps taken when the models are run with the protocols obtained from students. In addition to their contributions to cognitive science, it was thought that these models could serve as more explicit guides in the design of instructional materials and teaching.

The main theoretical concepts used in these analyses are a problem space of states, goals, and operators; a process of understanding that constructs problem representations; and schemata that organize the process of representation and planning solutions. Models have been developed for three general kinds of problems: problems that are solved by applying procedures, problems that are solved primarily through search or planning, and problems that depend primarily on representations.

Procedure-Based Problem Solving

Brown and Burton (1978) developed a model of cognitive procedures for solving computational exercises in subtraction. The goal of this work was to explain the errors that occur in children's performance of subtraction, as well as their correct responses, with a generative theory. The initial model by Brown and Burton had the form of a model for correct performance that accounted for errors by deleting components of the correct procedure. A program that diagnoses students' procedures from their performance on a special test was developed by Burton (1982). A simpler model (Young & O'Shea, 1981) in the form of production rules accounts for some of the errors that occur by deletion of productions. A later analysis by Brown and Van Lehn (1980) accounted for errors by assuming that part of the correct procedure had been learned, and local problem-solving heuristics are applied when work on a problem leads to an impasse. Subsequently, VanLehn (1983) provided an analysis of learning cognitive procedures from examples that predicts the kinds of incomplete knowledge that students acquire from the examples they encounter in the curriculum.

In algebra, analyses of errors in equation solving have been provided by Sleeman (1982), using a diagnostic system that assumes that students have acquired incorrect rules. Anderson (1988) has analyzed errors in algebra with a model consisting of production rules and an assumption that incorrect rules result from generalizations that allow rules to be applied incorrectly.

Problem Solving by Search and Planning Schemata

In geometry, a proof exercise presents a goal and given information, and the goal is reached through a series of inferential steps. This fits the form of problems solved by means-ends analysis by the General Problem Solver (GPS; Newell & Simon, 1972). In geometry problems, however, the main method of GPS for setting goals is not available. GPS solves symbolic problems such as logic by comparing the given or derived expression with the goal expression. noting differences, and setting a goal to remove one of the differences. In geometry, differences between expressions are not the point of the problem; rather, the given expressions are used to infer different expressions, eventually leading to inference of the goal expression.

In models of geometry problem solving (Anderson, 1982; Greeno, 1978) requirements include knowledge for setting goals based on information in the problem state. This strategic knowledge is specific to the domain of geometry. It includes knowledge for setting specific goals as well as indefinite goals such as "find a pattern of congruent parts that will prove that these two triangles are congruent" (Greeno, 1978). It also includes schemata that are activated by recognition of patterns of information in the problem and leads to selection of a plan for the problem, such as "try proving that these two triangles are congruent" or "use relations between angles formed by parallel lines" (Greeno, Magone, & Chaiklin, 1979; Lewis & Anderson, 1985). These plan schemata also provide a basis for adding lines to the problem diagram, using knowledge that identifies missing components from patterns that are needed for a plan to be applied (Greeno et al., 1979).

Anderson (1982) has provided a model that simulates the learning of procedural knowledge for geometry proof exercises. The learning processes for geometry are examples of processes that Anderson assumes occur generally in acquisition of cognitive skill: proceduralization, generalization, discrimination, and compilation.

Bundy (1975) gave an analysis of solving equations in algebra that identified strategies such as isolating the unknown variable and combining terms that contain the same variable.

Representation of Problems

Models of solution of word problems in arithmetic and algebra have been developed. The main theoretical idea used in these analyses is that of understanding language based on schemata. The schemata organize information in the problems in a way that enables the problem solver to choose operations to solve the problem or to formulate an equation that can then be solved.

Models of solving elementary arithmetic word problems were developed by Riley, Greeno and Heller (1983) and by Briars and Larkin (1984). The representations used by Riley et al. are similar to characterizations of addition and subtraction problems by Carpenter and Moser (1982), Nesher (1982), and Vergnaud (1982). Kintsch and Greeno (1985) modeled processes of text comprehension that lead to representations like those assumed by Riley et al. In the Riley et al. model, information in word problems is represented according to schemata for sets with specifications, kinds of objects, and quantities. These representations are related according to higher-order schemata that represent increases or decreases in set sizes, combinations of sets, and comparisons between sets. The model simulates problem-solving actions involving construction of models of the problem situation using blocks. Briars and Larkin's model links text propositions directly with problem-solving actions of model construction, and includes schema-based representations for more complex problems. An empirical analysis by Riley and Greeno (1988) has shown that the set-based model gave a successful account of problems involving changes and combinations, but that performance on problems involving comparisons was not explained well with this model.

Representations of algebra word problems have been studied by Hall, Kibler, Wenger, and Truxaw (in press). The characterization by these authors involves patterns of quantities with relations that can be represented graphically, with lengths of lines corresponding to extensive quantities such as distances and durations, and slopes of lines corresponding to intensive quantities such as speeds. A model of the process of understanding problems that Hall is developing simulates the construction of graphical representations based on problem texts.

USES OF COGNITIVE MODELS FOR INSTRUCTION

Cognitive models of problem solving have been used for instruction in school mathematics in three quite different ways. One use has been the incorporation of a model of successful problem solving in intelligent tutoring systems. A second use has been a basis for representations in computational learning environments. A third use has been to teach mathematics teachers about the cognitive processes hypothesized in a model.

"Expert" Models in Intelligent Tutoring Systems

Many intelligent tutoring systems include models of correct performance on problems. As a student works on a problem, the program compares steps that the student takes with its representation of a correct solution. This enables immediate feedback to the student if his or her solution departs from the solution that the "expert" model simulates.

A tutor of this kind was developed by Anderson, Boyle, and Yost (1985) for geometry proof exercises. The tutoring system uses the cognitive model of geometry problem solving that Anderson (1982) developed in two ways. One use is to provide a representation of the state of a student's work on the problem in the form of a graph showing the goals and inferences that have been made. This provides the student with an explicit representation of relations in the problem space that usually are implicit. The other use is as an "expert" model. If the student makes an incorrect inference, the tutoring program intervenes immediately and corrects the student's error, and if the student asks for help, the program provides a hint in terms of the "expert" model's goals at that time.

Other tutoring systems that incorporate a model of correct performance viewed as a cognitive skill include a program for instruction for solving algebra equations by McArthur, Stasz, Hotta, Peter, and Burdoff (1987).

Representations in Learning Environments

Cognitive models of problem solving have also been used to provide students with representations in learning environments that are exploratory, rather than didactic. Thompson (1988) has developed a program that enables students to construct semantic networks corresponding to arithmetic word problems. Thompson's system is an extension of an earlier program developed by Shalin and Bee (see Greeno, 1986; Greeno, Brown, Shalin, Bee, Lewis, & Vitolo, 1985) which used ideas in the cognitive model of understanding word problems that had been worked out by Carpenter and Moser (1982), Nesher (1982), Riley et al., (1983), and Vergnaud (1982). The computer program is a graphics editor that provides boxes corresponding to different types of quantities and allows a student to include various labels in each box as well as to construct links between the boxes for quantities that are related. Shalin and Bee's system extended the ideas in the models of addition and subtraction problems to include types of quantities and relations involving multiplication and division. Thompson's system adds labels for units, a feature used in Schwartz's (1982) Semantic Calculator, and propagates quantitative values according to appropriate arithmetic operations.

The instructional goal of Thompson's program is to provide explicit representations of information in problems that students must understand in order to succeed in solving the problem, but that is usually not explicit. This draws students' attention to features of problem information they might otherwise not be cognizant of and provides a visible representation that students can talk about with teachers and other students that refers to features of problem information that they need to understand.

Another program that provides explicit representations for students is Algebraland (Foss, 1987). This program was developed from ideas about strategic solutions of equations, proposed by Bundy (1975). Algebraland presents the student with a menu of operations, such as adding something to both sides of an equation, and provides a graph of steps taken during work on the problem. The graph can be annotated to indicate strategic goals that the student had at each of the steps. A display is constructed as the student works on a problem, and the student can review the steps that he or she took at any time during the effort, or after the problem has been solved. Like Thompson's program, Algebraland displays information explicitly that is ordinarily implicit in the problem-solving process. The displays given by Algebraland differ from those given by Thompson's program in that Algebraland displays a trace of the student's work in setting goals and applying operators, while Thompson's displays represent the student's understanding of the problem's informational structure. The display provided in the geometry tutor of Anderson et al. (1985) is like Algebraland in providing a trace of problem-solving goals and operations that a student can reflect on, but the geometry tutor differs from Algebraland in that it intervenes to keep a student on a track that its "expert" model can recognize as efficiently progressive toward the goal, while Algebraland simply keeps track of what the student does and gives the student something to think about.

Representations for Teaching

Cognitive analyses of problem solving have been used in an impressive way for teacher education by Carpenter, Fennema, Peterson, Chiang, and Loef (in press). Carpenter et al. used the ideas about children's understanding of arithmetic word problems developed by Carpenter and Moser (1982), Nesher (1982), Riley et al. (1983), and Vergnaud (1982) in a workshop for teachers. Explanations of the different kinds of addition and subtraction problems were given, and different ways that children can think about problems were explained. Teachers watched videotapes of children solving problems in different ways, focusing their attention on the methods of thinking, rather than on the answers given. Subsequent observations of the teachers in their classroom work showed that they had changed their practice of teaching significantly. They attended more to the methods that students used in solving problems, and were more sensitive to the difficulties that students had in understanding problems than comparable teachers who had not been in the workshop.

ACTIVITIES OF KNOWING AND LEARNING MATHEMATICS

The models of problem solving discussed in the first section were made possible by the view of cognition as symbolic information processing. In this section I discuss that view and its implications for framing assumptions about mathematical problem solving and reasoning in school.

The issue is how we view models of problem solving in relation to what we want students to learn in their mathematical education. One view is that students should learn to solve the problems that they are given in their instruction. According to that view, the models of problem solving that we develop are hypotheses about the knowledge we want students to acquire. We could treat these models as blueprints or circuit diagrams for the knowledge that the students should be acquiring. Then instruction could be organized so that students' performance would be made as close as possible to the performance of a model of successful problem solving. Indeed, that is the way in which "expert" problem-solving models are used in intelligent tutoring systems of the kind that Anderson et al. (1985) have developed.

Another view is that the problems that are used in school instruction should be means to more ambitious educational goals, rather than being the goals themselves. We hope that students will be able to reason effectively about mathematical concepts and principles and will be able to reason with mathematical concepts and principles about the events and systems that they encounter in their lives. On this view, learning mathematics involves acquiring aspects of an intellectual practice, rather than just acquiring some information and skills. Some aspects of this view are highlighted in discussions of mathematical problem solving by mathematicians (e.g., Polya, 1954; Schoenfeld, 1985). The view is also informed by considering mathematical learning as a kind of cognitive apprenticeship, where students are learning to engage in a kind of activity that is modeled and exemplified in the classroom setting (Collins, Brown, & Newman, in press; Lave, Smith, & Butler, in press). Important aspects of the view are also provided by considering mathematical knowledge as it is embodied in the practice of the mathematical community (e.g., Kitcher, 1984; Toulmin, 1972), rather than as it is encoded in mathematical writings.

If we view one of the goals of education as fostering capabilities for activities of mathematical thinking and reasoning, it becomes important to consider the situated character of mathematical knowing. Like all cognition, mathematical reasoning and understanding occurs in situations. In a view that is emerging from studies of expertise (e.g., Dreyfus & Dreyfus, 1986), analyses of technology in social contexts (e.g., Suchman, 1987; Winograd & Flores, 1986), and ethnographic investigations of cognition in work (e.g., Carraher, Carraher & Schliemann, 1985; Lave, 1988; Zuboff, 1988), some of us are becoming convinced that we need to treat the concept of knowing relativistically, analogous to the concept of motion in physics (Brown, in press; Greeno, 1989a, 1989b). This view of knowledge is analagous to the way that motion is understood relativistically in physics. That is, the properties of someone's knowing cannot be specified independently of the situation that provides a frame of reference for the person's cognitive activity, much as a physicist cannot specify properties of the motion of an object, independently of a frame of reference. The knowing of mathematics is situated in social and intellectual communities of practice, and for their mathematical knowing to be active and useful, individuals either must learn to act and reason mathematically in the settings of their practice or they must acquire capabilities to generate mathematical meaning and solutions of problems in situations that they encounter.

If we view mathematical cognition in this way, we are led to a pessimistic assessment of most current educational practice. A mathematics classroom is itself a determining context for the activities of students. The activities that dominate the practice of learning by students in classrooms are listening to what an authoritative teacher tells them, watching the teacher perform procedures, and learning to mimic the procedures that the teacher and textbook present. Successful learning includes adaptation to the requirements of the learning environment, and often does not go beyond such adaptation. Students who adapt successfully to the requirements of mathematics classrooms learn to listen, watch, and mimic effectively. If we believe that these receptive forms of activity are insufficient as outcomes of mathematics education, we may be forced to consider fundamental changes in the kinds of activity that students engage in as they learn mathematics.

Symbols and Meaning in Mathematics

One problematic aspect of learning mathematics results from the strong role that symbols play in mathematical reasoning. Activities in mathematics classrooms are dominated by manipulation of symbols. These symbols are intended to have meaning, of course, but they refer to abstract entities that are absent from the cognitive worlds of students.

To think about these issues, it is helpful to frame them in terms of some general concepts in the theory of symbols and representation. Figure 1 presents some of the relevant distinctions, in a form first presented by Smith (1983). The two rectangles on the left are the domain of symbolic expressions. The lower rectangle, labeled "symbolic notations," has sequences of characters that are well-formed according to the syntax of mathematical expressions. The upper rectangle, called "symbolic structures," has the expressions as they are organized by someone who understands them, including their constituent structure. The expression θ_s is a function that maps sequences of characters to structured expressions, and is approximately a parsing function.

The rounded rectangles on the right are the domain of things that the expressions are about. The lower rounded rectangle has objects and events — the things

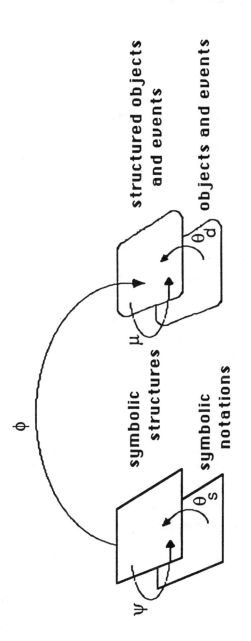

Figure 1. A view of semantics (after Smith, 1983).

that exist and the things that happen. The upper rounded rectangle has organized versions of those objects and events that are labeled "structured objects and events." The structures of objects and events include properties such as what things are parts of what other things, which objects are members of sets along with which other objects, which actions and events are parts of other actions and events, and so on.

ψ and μ are functions that take structures to other structures. ψ is a function that transforms symbolic expressions into other expressions. Operators in ψ include transformation between equivalent expressions or equations and rules of inference that justify writing new statements in a proof. μ is a function that transforms situations with objects and events into other situations. Its operators are the actions and processes that can occur in the world.

The most important entity in the diagram is ϕ. It is the mapping from the symbolic expressions to the objects and events that the expressions are about. For example, if there is an equation on the left side that is supposed to be about a relation between quantities in some process in the world, then the correspondence between the terms of the equation and the quantities involved in the process should be included in ϕ. A requirement on the construction of ψ, with an intended interpretation ϕ, is that when we perform operations on symbols that correspond to things that happen in the world, the symbolic expressions that result should describe the states that result from the real events.

Figure 2 shows a more elaborate version of the scheme, needed for thinking about mathematical systems. Sometimes we use mathematical expressions to describe processes and events in the world, as in the equations we use for word problems. Other times we use mathematical expressions to describe abstract entities and processes, such as sets, numbers, variables, and functions. Relations between concrete and abstract entities are much too complex to be captured by a pair of domains connected by an arrow, but this diagram at least recognizes that some of the uses of mathematical expressions involve denotations that are not directly in the physical world.

The goals of mathematics education are something like Figure 2, in which students know what the symbols can refer to in situations in the world, as well as in the domain of mathematical concepts and principles. In fact, getting something like Figure 2 into students' minds is not enough. We want them to be able to *construct* the ϕ relations for situations and concepts that they encounter. Unfortunately, all of this is probably beyond what most students acquire in their mathematics instruction. The outcome of school mathematics learning for most students is more like Figure 3, where the only meaning that symbolic structures have is in the symbolic notations themselves. The symbols are supposed to denote physical quantities or conceptual entities, but their referents are just notations — marks on paper or a chalk board. This is a perverse kind of knowledge, and a gross distortion of the epistemology of mathematics, but there is considerable evidence that many students come away from their classroom experience in mathematics with little more than a set of rules for manipulating symbols, which they can verify only by comparing the answers they get to symbolic problems with answers that are prescribed by teachers and textbooks.

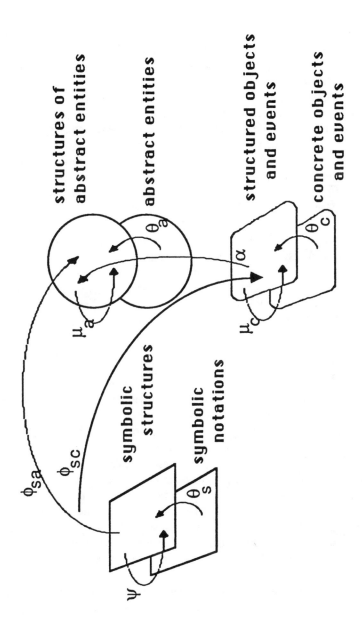

Figure 2. A view of semantics with abstract realities.

Beliefs and Understandings about Mathematical Knowing

As bad as these misconceptions about the meaning of mathematics are, they may not be the most serious consequences of our present mode of instruction. There are broader issues of mathematical epistemology for which current instructional practice has equally negative effects that are even more worrisome than those of mistakenly believing that mathematics is about its symbols.

The issues have been studied by Belenky, Clinchy, Goldberger, and Tarule (1986) and by Dweck (Dweck & Bempechat, 1983; Dweck & Leggett, 1988). They involve beliefs and understandings that individuals have and come to have about themselves as knowing agents and about their capabilities for learning and knowing.

The study conducted by Belenky et al. focused on the epistemological positions of individuals engaged in different kinds of learning institutions, including colleges and human service agencies that provide assistance and information for parents. They distinguished several epistemological positions involving quite different orientations toward learning and knowing. In one quite primitive orientation, called received knowing, one only obtains knowledge from authoritative sources. Learning is passive and assimilative, and the warrants for knowledge are the alleged authority of sources. Belenky et al. contrasted received knowing with more active epistemological positions, including subjective knowing, where the individual passes information and opinions through a personal filter; procedural knowing where the individual understands knowledge to be the product of cognitive or social processes; and constructive knowing, which results from a flexible combination of cognitive and social processes.

Dweck's research (e.g., Dweck & Bempechat, 1983; Dweck & Leggett, 1988) has also been concerned with individuals' beliefs and attitudes about knowing and learning. She has studied children's beliefs about what is involved in being "smart" and has related these beliefs to the children's causal attributions regarding their successes and failures and to their orientations and tendencies to engage in intellectual tasks. Dweck's research shows that some children understand intelligence as a fixed entity while other children understand intelligence as a set of capabilities that they strengthen by engaging in challenging intellectual tasks. The entity theorists view intellectual tasks as occasions in which their (fixed) amounts of intelligence will be evident to other persons and are attracted to easy tasks in which they can display a high level of performance. When they fail, they tend to blame their low level of ability, and they tend to explain their success on easy tests or luck. The malleable-trait theorists view intellectual tasks as opportunities for cognitive growth, and are attracted to challenging tasks in which they can improve their skills. When they fail, they tend to blame the tests or other situational factors, and they explain their success by their high ability and outstanding effort. These patterns are summarized as helplessness and mastery by the children whose beliefs involve fixed entities and malleable traits, respectively.

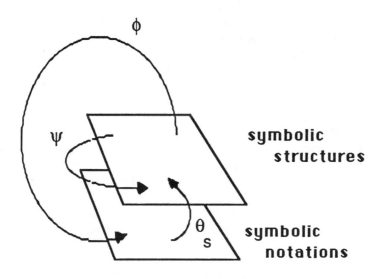

Figure 3. An unintended outcome of "good" instruction.

There has been very little research addressed to the question of how individuals develop the epistemological beliefs and understandings that they have. Even so, it may be reasonable to speculate on the effects that different classroom practices may have on the epistemologies that children develop, both at a general level and with respect to specific domains of knowledge, such as mathematics.

In most school instruction, what students mostly do is listen, watch, and mimic things that the teacher and textbook tell them and show them. If students' epistemologies are influenced at all by the experiences they have, then most students probably learn that mathematical knowledge is a form of received knowledge, not something that is constructed either personally or socially. Another probable outcome for many students is a belief that they were endowed with a low level of mathematical ability and that there is little or nothing they can do to become mathematically able. The links between classroom experiences and students' personal epistemologies undoubtedly are subtle and complex, and classroom experience undoubtedly is just one factor in determining what students believe about mathematical knowledge and about themselves as mathematical knowers and learners. Even so, it seems likely that the influence of current classroom practices on the epistemological beliefs and understandings of most students is largely negative.

The picture that I have drawn of ordinary classroom instruction is rather bleak. If things are this bad, how is it that any students learn and understand mathematics successfully? One possibility is that the teachers and students who achieve significant learning do so in spite of the situation they are in. There is a natural human tendency to make things meaningful if at all possible. Some teachers and students come to the classroom with strong beliefs and desires that mathematical symbols must mean something, and they manage to find ways to construct meaningful knowing of mathematics even with the weak support of meaning that is provided in the curriculum and the learning situation. According to their personal epistemologies, mathematical symbols are meaningful, and they act according to these beliefs even if they do not have explicit conceptual means for expressing the beliefs. Those few students who succeed in constructing meaning in spite of the routine character of mathematical knowledge in the classroom probably see themselves, correctly, as exceptionally talented, and see mathematical knowledge as a product of lonely and idiosyncratic creativity.

ALTERNATIVE CLASSROOM PRACTICES

Most current instruction in mathematics is didactic, treating mathematical knowing as a body of content and skills that teachers and textbooks present and that students are required to ingest and absorb. A view that mathematical knowing is an activity of reasoning about and with mathematical concepts and principles requires a different kind of learning activity by students. Two kinds of alternatives to the normal didactic practice of mathematical teaching have been developed and discussed in published reports. I will briefly discuss five examples that illustrate the two alternatives at different levels of mathematical instruction.

Processes of Problem Solving

In one kind of classroom activity, students are engaged in authentic mathematical problem solving. In these classrooms, mathematical problems provide occasions for reasoning and exploration. The main focus of the activity is on the processes of thinking and reasoning that are involved in mathematical work, rather than on whether students have learned how to get correct answers. Classroom teaching focused on problem-solving processes has been described by Schoenfeld (1986) regarding his course in mathematical problem solving for college students, and by Fennema, Carpenter, Keith, and Jenkins (1989) regarding second-grade mathematics classes.

Schoenfeld's teaching focuses on college students' epistemological beliefs about mathematical knowing and learning, as well as on their developing capabilities for mathematical problem solving and understanding. One epistemological outcome of current teaching is a belief by students that mathematical problems are solved by applying procedures that a person may or may not know, and if the person has not solved a problem within a very few minutes (certainly no more than five) there is no point in continuing to try. Of course, mathematicians regularly work on problems that take many hours — indeed, if a question can be answered by mechanically applying a known procedure, mathematicians do not think it is a problem at all. Schoenfeld sets problems for his students to work on that require extended effort and engages in extended problem solving himself to engage students in genuine mathematical activity and thereby to learn to reason meaningfully about mathematical concepts and principles. He emphasizes that methods and approaches to problems need to be tried and evaluated, and that significant learning can occur through an attempt to solve a problem that does not succeed.

Fennema et al. (1989) described second-grade classrooms in which mathematical problem solving is an activity that students engage in enthusiastically, attending primarily to the methods they use rather than to the answers they get. Students formulate problems for themselves and each other to work on and write descriptions of the various methods that different students used to solve the problems. Fennema et al. reported that, by student demand, mathematical activity takes up more than an hour per day in their classes, rather than the usual 20-30 minutes.

Activities of Mathematical Discourse

Another approach to participatory mathematics teaching focuses on mathematical discourse and argumentation. Alibert (1988) described a first-year university course, Fawcett (1938) described a high-school geometry course, and Lampert (1986, 1988) described teaching fifth-grade mathematics in which the teacher and students engage in collaborative mathematical inquiry, offering and examining conjectures and assumptions.

Alibert (1988) and his colleagues described a course that focuses on development of co-didactic situations in which a student works to convince others and himself or herself of the truth of a conjecture that has been formulated in response to a general problem that the class is trying to solve. The course design includes developing didactic customs that are different from those of standard classroom activity, including extensive debates about conjectures, including proof arguments and counterexamples, that students address to each other in their efforts to arrive at conclusive opinions.

Fawcett's (1938) course in high-school geometry focused on mathematical proof. The class discussed alternative definitions and postulates, and each student was responsible for a formulation of concepts and assumptions in developing his or her personal version of the geometry, which was recorded in a notebook. Class activities included discussion of everyday materials including advertising claims and application of laws regarding issues of definition and implicit assumptions that would be needed for conclusions to follow from premises.

In Lampert's (1986, 1988) teaching of fifth-grade mathematics she builds a classroom participation structure in which the students and the teacher collaborate in their joint effort to make sense of mathematical concepts and procedures. As an example, Lampert (1988) presented a transcript of exchange that occurred as students were discussing the last digits of positive integers raised to different powers. They had previously determined that all the powers of 5 end in 5, and that the last digit of 7^4 is 1. Lampert then asked, "What about seven to the fifth power?" Students responded:

Arthur: I think it's going to be a 1 again.
Sarah: I think it's 9.
Soo Wo: I think it's going to be 7.
Sam: It is 7.

Lampert wrote on the board:

$$7^5 = 1?$$
$$9?$$
$$7?$$

She then said, "You must have a proof in mind, Sam, to be so sure," and asked, "Arthur, why do you think it's one?" The following discussion ensued:

Arthur: Because 7^4 ends in 1, then it's times 1 again.
Gar: The answer to 7^4 is 2401. You multiply that by 7 to get the answer, so it's 7 times 1.
Teacher: Why 9, Sarah?
Theresa: I think Sarah thought the number should be 49.
Gar: Maybe they think it goes 9, 1, 9, 1, 9, 1.
Molly: I know it's 7, 'cause 7...
Abdul: Because 7^4 ends in 1, so if you times it by 7, it'll end in 7.
Martha: I think it's 7. No, I think it's 8.

Sam: I don't think it's 8 because it's odd number times odd number and that's always an odd number.

Carl: It's 7 because it's like saying 49 times 49 times 7.

Arthur: I still think it's 1 because you do 7 times 7 to get 49 and then for 7^4 you do 49 times 49 and for 7^5 I think you'll do 7^4 times itself and that will end in one.

Teacher: What's 49^2 ?

Soo Wo: 2401.

Teacher: Arthur's theory is that 7^5 should be 2401 times 2401 and since there's a 1 here and a 1 here...

Soo Wo: It's 2401 times 7.

Gar: I have a proof that it won't be a 9. It can't be 9, 1, 9, 1, because 7^3 ends a 3.

Martha: I think it goes 1, 7, 9, 1, 7, 9, 1, 7, 9,.

Teacher: What about 7^3 ending in 3? The last number ends in...9 times 7 is 63.

Martha: Oh...

Karl: Abdul's thing isn't wrong, 'cause it works. He said times the last digit by 7 and the last digit is 9, so the last one will be 3. It's 1, 7, 9, 3, 1, 7, 9, 3.

Arthur: I want to revise my thinking. It would be 7 times 7 times 7 times 7 times 7. I was thinking it would be 7 times 7 times 7 times 7 times 7 times 7 times 7 times 7.

Teacher: What power's *that* ?

Arthur: Eighth.

The conversation continued with some discussion of the squares of numbers raised to powers. (1988, p. 459)

This example from Lampert's (1988) teaching, like many others discussed by Alibert (1988), Fawcett (1938), Fennema et al. (1989), and Schoenfeld (1986), illustrates mathematical problem solving of a very different kind than the problem solving that is characterized in information-processing models that simulate solutions of text problems. Work on a problem consists of having a conversation. The goal of the activity is to reach a better understanding of something, rather than to construct a pre-specified state in a space of symbolic expressions. The operators are conversational acts that contribute information and ideas to the body of shared opinions, reasons, and explanations that the group has constructed.

An important feature of these conversations is that they include metacognitive topics as well as topics directly in the subject matter. Students are concerned with the processes they are using in thinking about problems, and these processes are considered explicitly in the conversations. There is no clear and simple distinction between discussions about numbers and other mathematical entities and discussions about adequacy of arguments, reasons for opinions, and processes of thinking. This is appropriate, because mathematics in these classrooms is an activity of intellectual inquiry, and while this activity depends on an existing body of content, it is not limited to transmitting that content. Indeed, the educational conversations continually extend the body of mathematical practice for the social group that is involved.

Roles of Research Results in Alternative Educational Practices

Models of problem solving that have been developed in cognitive/educational research can be used as templates of student performance, but that is not their only possible use. The results of research about arithmetic word problem solving were used by Carpenter et al. (in press) in a teacher-education workshop, and the teachers consequently attended more to children's methods of problem solving. In the practice that they developed, teachers came to encourage variability in the children's methods and discussions of the various ways that problems can be solved. One can imagine a quite different way in which the models could have been used— as defining instructional templates that might have improved children's performance on tests without providing them with opportunities to reflect on their understanding or occasions to enjoy generating alternative approaches.

Alternative uses can also be made of computational systems that grow out of research on mathematical problem solving. Thompson's (1988) system that enables construction of semantic networks for word problems could be used in quite different ways by teachers. If teachers use the system as a way for students to explicate their understandings of problem situations and as a vehicle for discussing general properties of numerical and quantitative operations, it can facilitate the development of mathematical discourse and enrich students' ability to participate in meaningful knowing and learning. It could also be used to prescribe outcomes of cognitive processes so that students were required to learn how to produce the correct diagrams for problems, rather than merely being required to produce correct answers, as they are now.

Systems that display traces of students' problem-solving steps such as those of Anderson et al. (1985) and Algebraland (Foss, 1987) also are susceptible to quite different uses. The Anderson et al. computational tutor uses the traces to help students recognize appropriate goals and relations between goals and problem-solving operations as an aid to their learning to correctly solve proof exercises. Algebraland's display system is not built into a tutor and has been used in research (Foss, 1987) as an invitation for students to reflect on the sequence of steps they carried out. Either of these graphical displays could be used quite differently as objects that can facilitate discussions about alternative proofs or solution paths, including invariant features as well as variable features of solutions and their relations to mathematical properties of the problems and solution methods.

AN ENLARGED RESEARCH AGENDA

Cognitive research has provided understanding of problem solving in mathematics to a significant but limited extent. We can characterize cognitive structures and processes required for solving routine text problems; several examples have been worked out, and continuing research can provide analyses of text problem solving throughout the school curriculum. On the other hand, some important issues about problem solving have not been addressed in the mainstream research, and a broadening of the research agenda could be productive for theory as well as being helpful for educational practice.

In most research done until now, problem solving has been treated as an autonomous activity. That is atypical in ordinary cognitive life. Ordinarily, solution of a problem is instrumental for something else. Lave (1988) has made the point that in everyday cognition, problems are dilemmas that arise in the structure of an activity. The same is true in intellectual work. Problems that we work on in research or that are productive in learning are important because their solutions contribute to the growth of knowledge and understanding.

A new direction in research is needed so we can begin to understand how problem solving is structured by its context and how it contributes to other goals. One major dimension of this research would be to study problem solving in contexts of learning and conceptual growth. This would include studying problem solving in social contexts of learning, including the kinds of mathematics classrooms that Alibert (1988), Fawcett (1938), Fennema et al. (1989), Lampert (1988), and Schoenfeld (1986) have described. It also would include study of consequences for students' epistemological beliefs and understandings about mathematics of different ways in which problem solving occurs in learning contexts.

A Situation for Learning and Knowing About Functions

One aspect of this research agenda is study of students' abilities to reason mathematically in situations using resources other than procedures and schemata that they have acquired in direct instruction. Studies of quantitative reasoning in everyday situations have begun to provide information that complements studies of problem solving in school tasks (e.g., Carraher et al., 1985; Lave, 1989; Saxe, 1988; Scribner, 1984). Another aspect of the problem can be studied in situations that are novel to individuals, but are organized so they can be understood easily.

Along with a group of colleagues and students, I have begun a project that I hope will contribute to this research direction. The group includes Joyce Moore, Meg Korpi, Jean-Luc Gurtner, Greg Pribyl, Richard Mander, Jan Kerkhoven, Rachelle Hackett, Jonathan Simon, and Allison Kelly. The situation that we present to students is a machine in which quantities are related by linear functions. The research is focused on three general questions, each of which has a theoretical side and a side related to educational practice.

The first question is the nature of students' implicit understanding or conceptual competence regarding variables and functions. This relates to general theoretical questions in cognitive science about understanding that is functional but implicit (e.g., Gelman & Greeno, in press; Greeno, Riley & Gelman, 1984), and to the practical question of the feasibility of learning in which students discuss and refine mathematical concepts and principles that are important for understanding algebra, rather than simply receiving them.

The second question involves characteristics of situations in which implicit understanding of functions is effective. A theoretical position is being developed (e.g., Brown, in press; Greeno, 1988a, 1988b) in which cognition is viewed as being relativistically dependent on situations. On this view, the analysis of situations that enable effective reasoning addresses a fundamental question for cognitive science. In the research that I discuss here, the question involves identifying characteristics of a situation in which students can reason effectively about functional relations among quantities. The practical side of this question involves possible designs for materials and activities that could be used in instruction in algebra.

The third question that is addressed in this research is about language. The language issues are not issues about students' understanding of formal mathematics. Rather, they involve uses of terms in ordinary language that refer to quantities that are properties or relations in the situation that we use to exemplify functions. One aspect of a view of situated cognition is that meanings of terms are products of the communicative activity of persons in a situation, reached by a process of collaboration, and this production of meaning occurs frequently in the situation that we are studying. The practical side of this issue relates to the role of language in learning. In teaching mathematics, we often begin by giving students definitions of terms, and then we expect them to use the terms correctly because "they should know what the words mean." Formal definitions have an important role in mathematics, of course, but we also need to create situations for students to communicate about with them.

Method. In our research, we ask students to reason about the operation of a simple machine, sketched in Figure 4. The machine is a board, about a yard long, with two grooves that run lengthwise. Beside each groove is a ruler, marked in inches. Each groove holds a small metal block with a pointer on its top surface. A string is tied to each block. At the end of each groove there is an axle attached to a wheel with a handle so the axle can be turned. Metal sleeves can be placed on the two axles, and the sleeves differ in circumference. The two axles can be linked together so they turn simultaneously, or they can be separated so they turn independently.

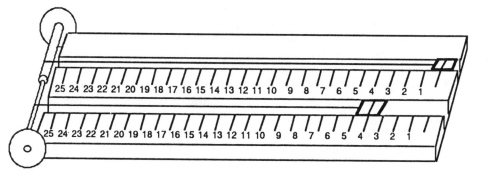

Figure 4.

The device is an embodiment of linear functions. Think of the formula $y = mx + b$. The term y is where the block is after you turn a handle some number of times. The term b is where the block was when you started counting the turns. The term m is the circumference of the spool you used. And x is the number of times you turned the handle. As we have used the machine, the functions all have positive slopes of 2, 3, 4, or 6, with values of y between zero and 30 or so.

In terms of Figure 2, we designed the machine as a concrete physical system with the main physical operation of pulling blocks along the tracks by turning the handle or handles. We hoped that functional relations between the quantities in the situation (e.g., the relation between number of turns and distance moved) would be obvious to students and would correspond to some abstract entities that they would reason about. In our first study, we made no effort to include the standard symbolic expressions of algebra. Some students made use of mathematical symbols, usually in the form of tables. Mainly though, the symbolic expressions involved in our situation are in ordinary English.

In a preliminary study, we interviewed students in pairs, either two girls or two boys. In most cases, the students who were interviewed together were friends. The interviews were about 40 minutes long. First, the students became familiar with the machine; they used different spools and starting points for a single track, and they talked about what happened. In the second part of the interview, situations were set up by the interviewer with blocks started at specified places in the two tracks, spools of specified sizes, and the axles specified to be linked or independent. For each situation, students were asked three open-ended questions : (1) What will happen when you turn the handle (or handles)? (2) What can you say about how far apart the blocks will be? (3) What can you say about where the blocks will be when you stop turning?

In the third part of the interview, situations were described and the students were asked how to make them happen. First, students were asked how to make one of the blocks get to 20 before the other block. Next, they were asked how to make the two blocks get to 24 at the same time. In each case they were asked to give three solutions, with constraints added to prevent the same combination of equal or unequal variables.

In the fourth section of the interview the students were asked a series of questions requiring inferences based on the linear functions in some situations. For one question the red block had a 3-spool and started at 10, the blue block had a 4-spool and started at 5, and the axles were linked. Students were asked how many turns it would take for the blue block to catch up with the red block. For another series of questions, the red block had a 3-spool, the blue block had a 6-spool, the axles were linked, and the blocks started at zero. Students were asked whether the red block would ever get ahead, how far ahead the blue block would be after four turns, whether the blue block would ever be ahead by six inches, whether the number of the blue block's position (called "the number the block is at") would ever be twice the number of the red block's position, or three times the number of the red block's position. A similar series of questions was asked for a situation with the same spool sizes, but with the red block starting at nine and the blue block at zero.

Finally, students were asked a question designed to elicit discussion in general terms: "Imagine that blue is going to start behind red by some amount, but I won't tell you the amount, and blue has a bigger spool than red, but I won't tell you the spool sizes. The axles have to be linked. What can you say about when blue will catch up with red?"

We had interviews with ten pairs of students. Four pairs were seventh-grade students who had not studied algebra at all. Three pairs were ninth-grade students at the end of their first course in algebra. And three pairs were eleventh-grade students at the end of their second course in algebra.

Illustrative Findings. I will present two examples from the transcriptions of interviews that illustrate general features of our results. The first example is from an interview with seventh-grade students in a situation where the red block had a 3-inch spool, the blue block had a 6-inch spool, and both blocks were started at point 0 (the far ends of the tracks). Mathematically, the situation can be described as two functions of a single variable: $f1(x) = 3x$ (the red block) and $f2(x) = 6x$ (the blue block). The students had already correctly answered the question: "When you turn the handle, will the red block ever get ahead?" Then they were asked, "How far ahead will the blue block be after four turns?" One of the students, ST2, gave the correct answer quickly, saying, "Six times four is 24 and half of 24 is 12." Then the following exchange ensued.

> ST1: I have something else: One turn is three inches, and three times four...
> ST2: That was on a different thing, though.
> ST1: Let's see — (to INT) what was it we were trying to get?
> INT: The question was, how far ahead will the blue be after you make four turns. And they're linked.
> ST1: Ah, I think 11. It's so close — I don't want to (motion to ST2).

(We think that ST1 thought it would be better not to give the same answer as ST2 had already given.)

> INT: Oh, you can copy him; I mean, I want you guys to work together.
> ST1: Ok, I say 12 too, then.
> INT: (to ST1) How did you figure, did you figure out 12, you think, a different way than he did?
> ST1: Yeah, well, I figured out three, ok, one turn is three, and then
> INT: Three for what?
> ST1: One turn it'll go three inches.
> ST2: (ST1's name), that was for a different thing. You don't know what it is for a six.
> INT: Well, the six is six inches, for a turn.
> ST1: Oh, it is? Oh yeah, huh. So six times— (laughs)— uh, 12.
> ST2: I figured out six inches— six divided by three is two, um, and then 12 times three, I mean 12 times two is 24—I don't know how I did it (shrugs).
> INT: OK.
> ST2: Let's try it. (turns handle)
> INT: Are you counting turns?
> ST2: Oops. (ST2, ST1, and INT reset the machine, run the trial again.)
> ST1: I think, in four turns? 24. I think 24.
> INT: 24 apart?
> ST1: [something inaudible]
> ST2: Ah, now we changed it.
> ST1: 24.
> ST2: OK, 24? (Count, pointing to positions from blue's position at 24 back toward red's position at 12) one, two, three, four, five, six, seven, eight —

> ST1: Oh, like that!
> ST2: Nine, 10, 11, 12, 13, about— 12, maybe.
> ST1: Oh, I thought 24, about how far it would go.
> INT: OK, so you were —
> ST1: I didn't know it was 12 in between. I thought it was — who would get to 12 first, in four turns. Oh, no!

The other example that I present was obtained in the third section of the interview, when two eleventh-grade students were asked how to make the two blocks get to 24 at the same time. ST3 proposed linking the axles, putting a 4-spool on each axle, and turning the handle six times. Then the interviewer asked for another solution.

INT: OK, so everything's equal, right? OK, how about if, let's say I have an unequal starting point, one starts ahead of the other.
ST4: Put one —
ST3: Put a —
ST4: — at 6, one at 3, turn one 8, turn one 4.
INT: OK, can you figure out a specific answer. I'm sorry, maybe I missed that one. What was—
ST3: I think you just said —
ST4: You put one, put one, OK give it the spool of 3.
INT: OK.
ST4: Put it at, um, where are you going to put it at?
ST3: Eight.
ST4: No, I screwed up.
ST3: No, you gotta take a spool —
ST4: Put one at 8, right?
ST3: Put one at 8.
ST4: And then turn that three times with the 3 spool (puts the block on ST2's side at 8).
INT: OK, we're trying to tie at 24.
ST4: Trying to tie at 24. All right, so put this one at 4 (puts the block on ST1's side at 4).
ST3: Put a 6-spool on it.
ST4: Turn it four times—no, you need to turn it six times. And then you're tied at 24.
ST3: With a — yeah.
ST4: With a —
ST3: But would we tie? Would we be there at the same time?
ST4: If we turn it slowly.
INT: You want to check that out?
ST3: But we don't have a 3-spool.
INT: Yeah you do, the small one's a 3.
ST3: Oh, OK.
ST4: Now wait; I get 6 — no, I get 3. (ST1 places a 6-spool on the axle; ST2 places a 3-spool on an axle.)
ST3: You're more mechanically inclined than I am.
INT: You said start this one where? (adjusts the block on ST2's side) At 8?
ST3: Eight, and this one (block on ST1's side at 4).

[ST3 and ST4 ask some questions about the reason for the study, the videotaping, and the mechanics of linking the axles.]

ST3: So these shouldn't be hooked up then, should they?

INT: Oh, it's up to you. You're constructing the situations. So you wanted this one to be at 8, right? OK, there's 8. (places ST2's block at 8) There's 4 (places ST1's block at 4). Now, you said —

ST4: Something's wrong.

INT: How many turns did you say?

ST4: Something's wrong.

INT: We're trying to tie —

ST4: What were we trying to get at again?

ST3: 24.

INT: We're trying to tie it right here (places a marker at 24).

ST4: It's not going to work.

INT: Why not? What's wrong?

ST4: I said, I screwed up; I said, um, you turn it, you have to turn it, you can't turn it an even, an even, I mean a whole number of times to get it to be eight.

INT: Oh, you don't have to turn a whole number of times.

ST4: Oh, just get it there?

INT: Yeah, well you have to tie at 24. That was the —

ST3: Do we have to turn it the same —

ST4: We both arrive at 24 at the same time?

INT: That's right, that's the only thing, that's your goal.

(Some further discussion about the problem, with ST2 expressing some negative feelings about what's going on.)

INT: What are you thinking?

ST4: I, if you put the 6 on, put it at the zero and turn four times, or put it at 12 and turn it two times.

INT: OK.

ST4: Or put it at 6 and turn it three times.

INT: Gotcha.

ST4: Then you'll make it, but then you'd have to get the 3, put it at, let's see if this (the 6-spool) takes — 4, 3'll take — 8. So put it halfway, so if we turn it equal number of times, so if I'm turning this (6-spool) four times and you turn this four times, three times four is 12, so put that at 12 (ST1's block), put this at zero (ST2's block), and turn 'em equal times.

(ST3 and ST4 then ran a trial, confirming that these conditions work.)

Discussion. All of the students that we interviewed were able to answer simple questions about the device, indicating that they had significant understanding of the functional relations among quantities in the situation.

The two examples illustrate interesting features of situated cognition. In the first example, ST2 understood the question as INT intended it and gave the correct answer right away. ST1, however, apparently was focused on the distance one block would move and discussed the distance that the red block would move in four turns.

Eventually, ST2 showed, by counting off inches between the positions of the blocks, that the quantity that he (and INT) had been discussing was the difference between the two positions. The difference between the positions was not a mysterious concept to ST1 — when he realized that the discrepancy had occurred he put his hand to his forehead in embarrassment — but the statement of the question initially had not succeeded in getting him focused on the same quantity that INT had intended.

Our interpretation of the second example is that ST4 was only weakly connected to the situation. He was acting quite bored. When the question was asked, getting both blocks to the position 24, ST4 generated two pairs of numbers with products of 24 (six times four and three times eight). This would have solved the problem if six and three were spool sizes and four and eight were numbers of turns. ST4, however, specified six and three as starting points. ST4 adjusted the solution by specifying different spool sizes. Eight became a starting point, with three both a spool size and a number of turns. The other block was placed at 4, and 6 was specified as both a spool size and a number of turns. The discussion, mainly by ST4, has the character of "playing with numbers," rather than reasoning about the quantities in the situation. Eventually, after a rather long excursion including a detour into a conversation about what the study was for, ST4 produced an analysis that was adequate to provide a solution. This happened after the machine had been set up with two spools and the handles were being turned. Therefore, it seems likely that the solution depended on being in the situation and observing the relations between quantities, although it is possible that it could have happened without the machine being physically present.

SUMMARY

I have reviewed the present state of research about problem solving in school mathematics. I believe this domain has provided information-processing theory with one of its major success stories. Information-processing models of solving school mathematics problems have provided significant understanding of procedure-based problem solving, problem solving that depends mainly on search and planning, and problem solving that depends primarily on success in representation using schemata. All these kinds of models have been used in the design of instruction.

These models can be considered in two ways. Considering them as objectives of instruction reflects a narrow view of learning in mathematics that involves acquiring skills and knowledge for solving pre-specified problems. Alternative classroom practices focus on students' understanding of processes and on the significance of problem solving and of learning to engage in mathematical discourse intended to increase a group's understanding of concepts and principles.

In these alternative educational practices, problem solving is not unimportant, but it does not constitute the major goal of the enterprise. Like problems about quantities in ordinary activity, problems in mathematics arise in a larger context that makes them meaningful. We could refocus our research effort toward problem solving in broader contexts, including the study of abilities of individuals to reason about quantities in situations they can understand. I have presented some preliminary findings from some research that I hope will contribute to that goal.

Acknowledgements

This research was supported by the National Science Foundation, grant BNS-8718918. This paper is based in part on an invited plenary presentation at the North American Chapter of the International Group for the Psychology of Mathematics Education, given at Northern Illinois University in 1988 and published in the proceedings of that meeting.

REFERENCES

Alibert, D. (1988). Towards new customs in the classroom. *For the Learning of Mathematics, 8*, 31-35, 43.

Anderson, J. R. (1982). Acquisition of cognitive skill. *Psychological Review, 89*, 396-406.

Anderson, J. R. (1988). The analogical origins of errors in problem solving. In D. Klahr & K. Kotovsky (Eds.), *Complex information processing* (pp. 343-370). Hillsdale, NJ: Lawrence Erlbaum Associates.

Anderson, J. R., Boyle, C. F., & Yost, G. (1985). The geometry tutor. In A. Joshi (Ed.), *Proceedings of the Ninth International Joint Conference on Artificial Intelligence* (p. 1-7). Los Altos, CA: Morgan Kaufmann.

Belenky, M. F., Clinchy, B. M., Goldberger, N. R., & Tarule, J. M. (1986). *Women's ways of knowing.* New York: Basic.

Briars, D. J., & Larkin, J. H. (1984). An integrated model of skill in solving elementary word problems. *Cognition and Instruction, 1*, 245-296.

Brown, J. S. (in press). Toward a new epistemology for learning. In C. Frasson & J. Gauthiar (Eds.), *Intelligent tutoring systems at the crossroad of AI and education.* Norwood, NJ: Ablex.

Brown, J. S., & Burton, R. R. (1978). Diagnostic models for procedural bugs in basic mathematical skills. *Cognitive Science, 2*, 155-192.

Brown, J. S., & VanLehn, K. (1980). Repair theory: A generative theory of bugs in procedural skills. *Cognitive Science, 4*, 379-426.

Bundy, A. (1975). Analyzing mathematical proofs (or reading between the lines). In P. Winston (Ed.), *Proceedings of the 4th International Joint Conference on Artificial Intelligence.* Cambridge, MA: Artificial Intelligence Laboratory.

Burton, R. R. (1982). Diagnosing bugs in a simple procedural skill. In D. Sleeman & J. S. Brown (Eds.), *Intelligent tutoring systems* (pp. 157-184). New York: Academic.

Carpenter, T. P., Fennema, E., Peterson, P. L., Chiang, C., & Loef, M. (in press). Using knowledge of children's mathematics thinking in classroom teaching: An experimental study. *American Educational Research Journal.*

Carpenter, T. P., & Moser, J. M. (1982). The development of addition and subtraction problem-solving skills. In T. P. Carpenter, J. M. Moser, & T. A. Romberg (Eds.), *Addition and subtraction: A cognitive perspective* (pp. 9-24). Hillsdale, NJ: Lawrence Erlbaum Associates.

Carraher, T. N., Carraher, D. W., & Schliemann, A. D. (1985). Mathematics in the streets and the schools. *British Journal of Developmental Psychology, 3,* 21-29.

Collins, A., Brown, J. S., & Newman, S. E. (in press). Cognitive apprenticeship: Teaching the craft of reading, writing, and mathematics. In L. B. Resnick (Ed.), *Knowing, learning, and instruction: Essays in honor of Robert Glaser* (pp. 453 - 494). Hillsdale, NJ: Lawrence Erlbaum Associates.

Dreyfus, H. L., & Dreyfus, S. E. (1986). *Mind over machine.* New York: The Free Press.

Dweck, C. & Bempechat, J. (1983). Children's theories of intelligence: Consequences for learning. In S. G. Paris, G. M. Olson, & H. W. Stevenson (Eds.), *Learning and motivation in the classroom* (pp. 239 - 256). Hillsdale, NJ: Lawrence Erlbaum Associates.

Dweck, C., & Legett, E. L. (1988). A social-cognitive approach to motivation and personality. *Psychological Review, 95,* 256-273.

Fawcett, H.P. (1938). *The nature of proof.* New York: Teachers' College, Columbia University.

Fennema, E., Carpenter, T., Keith, A., & Jenkins, M. (1989). *Cognitively guided instruction.* Presentation at the meeting of the American Educational Research Association, San Francisco.

Foss, C. L. (1987). Learning from errors in Algebraland (IRL Report IRL87-0003). Palo Alto, CA: Institute for Research on Learning.

Gelman, R., & Greeno, J. G. (in press). On the nature of competence: Principles for understanding in domains. In L. B. Resnick (Ed.), *Knowing, learning, and instruction: Essays in honor of Robert Glaser.* Hillsdale, NJ: Lawrence Erlbaum Associates.

Greeno, J. G. (1976). Cognitive objectives of instruction: Theory of knowledge for solving problems and answering questions. In D. Klahr (Ed.), *Cognition and instruction* (pp. 123-160). Hillsdale, NJ: Lawrence Erlbaum Associates.

Greeno, J. G. (1978). A study of problem solving. In R. Glaser (Ed.), *Advances in instructional psychology* (Vol. 1, pp. 13-75). Hillsdale, NJ: Lawrence Erlbaum Associates.

Greeno, J. G. (1986). Instructional representations based on research about understanding. In A. H. Schoenfeld (Ed.), *Cognitive science and mathematics education* (pp. 61-88). Hillsdale, NJ: Lawrence Erlbaum Associates.

Greeno, J. G. (1989a). A perspective on thinking. *American Psychologist, 44,* 134-141.

Greeno, J. G. (1989b). Situations, mental models, and generative knowledge. In D. Klahr & K. Kotovsky (Eds.), *Complex information processing: The impact of Herbert A. Simon* (pp. 285-318). Hillsdale, NJ: Lawrence Erlbaum Associates.

Greeno, J. G., Brown J. S., Foss, C., Shalin, V., Bee, N. V., Lewis, M. W., & Vitolo, T. M. (1985). *Cognitive principles of problem solving and computer-assisted instruction* (Tech. Rep. No. 154 - 497). University of Pittsburgh.

Greeno, J. G., Magone, M. E., & Chaiklin, S. (1979). Theory of constructions and set in problem solving. *Memory and Cognition, 7,* 445-461.

Greeno, J. G., Riley, M. S., & Gelman, R. (1984). Conceptual competence and young children's counting. *Cognitive Psychology, 16*, 44-143.
Hall, R., Kibler, D., Wenger, E., & Truxaw, C. (in press). Exploring the episodic structure of algebra story problem solving. *Cognition and Instruction.*
Kintsch, W., & Greeno, J. G. (1985). Understanding and solving word arithmetic problems. *Psychological Review, 92*, 109-129.
Kitcher, P. (1984). *The nature of mathematical knowledge.* New York: Oxford University Press.
Lampert, M. (1986). Knowing, doing, and teaching multiplication. *Cognition and Instruction, 3*, 305-342.
Lampert, M. (1988). The teacher's role in reinventing the meaning of mathematical knowing in the classroom. *Proceedings of the North American Chapter of the International Group for the Psychology of Mathematics Education.* DeKalb, IL: Northern Illinois University.
Lave, J. (1988). *Cognition in practice.* New York: Cambridge University Press.
Lave, J., Smith, S., & Butler, M. (in press). Problem solving as an everyday activity. In R. Charles & E. Silver (Eds.), *Teaching and measuring problem solving* (pp. 1 - 81). Reston, VA: National Council of Teachers of Mathematics.
Lewis, M.W., & Anderson, J. R. (1985). Discrimination of operator schemata in problem solving: Learning from examples. *Cognitive Psychology, 17*, 26-65.
McArthur, D., Stasz, C., Hotta, J. Y., Peter, O., & Burdorf, C. (1987). *Skill-oriented lesson control in an intelligent tutor for basic algebra.* Santa Monica, CA: The RAND Corporation.
Nesher, P. (1982). Levels of description in the analysis of addition and subtraction work problems. In T. P. Carpenter, J. M. Moser, & T. A. Romberg (Eds.), *Addition and subtraction: A cognitive perspective* (pp. 25-38). Hillsdale, NJ: Lawrence Erlbaum Associates.
Newell, A., & Simon, H. A. (1972). *Human problem solving.* Englewood Cliffs, NJ: Prentice-Hall.
Polya, G. (1954). *Induction and analogy in mathematics.* Princeton, NJ: Princeton University Press.
Riley, M. S., & Greeno, J. G. (1988). Developmental analysis of understanding language about quantities and of solving problems. *Cognition and Instruction, 5*, 49-101.
Riley, M. S., Greeno, J. G., & Heller, J. I. (1983). Development of children's problem-solving ability in arithmetic. In H. P. Ginsburg (Ed.), *The development of mathematical thinking* (pp. 153-196). New York: Academic.
Saxe, G. B. (1988). Candy selling and math learning. *Educational Researcher, 17*, 14-21.
Schoenfeld, A. H. (1985). *Mathematical problem solving.* New York: Academic.
Schoenfeld, A. H. (1986). What's all the fuss about metacognition? In A. H. Schoenfeld (Ed.), *Cognitive science and mathematics education* (pp. 189-216). Hillsdale, NJ: Lawrence Erlbaum Associates.
Scribner, S. (1984). Studying working intelligence. In B. Rogoff & J. Lave (Eds.), *Everyday cognition: Its development in social context* (pp. 9-40). Cambridge, MA: Harvard University Press.
Schwartz, J. (1982). The semantic calculator. *Classroom Computer News, 2*, 22-24.
Sleeman, D. (1982). Assessing aspects of competence in basic algebra. In D. Sleeman & J. S. Brown (Eds.), *Intelligent tutoring systems* (pp. 185-200). New York: Academic.
Smith, B. C. (1983). Reflection and semantics in a procedural language (Technical Report No. 22). Cambridge, MA: MIT, Laboratory for Computer Science.

Suchman, L. (1983). *Plans and situated actions.* NewYork: Cambridge University Press.

Thompson, P. W. (1988). Quantitative concepts as a foundation for algebraic reasoning: Sufficiency, necessity, and cognitive obstacles. *Proceedings of the North American Chapter of the International Group for the Psychology of Mathematics Education* (pp. 163-170). DeKalb, IL: Northern Illinois University.

Toulmin, S. (1972). *Human understanding.* Princeton, NJ: Princeton University Press.

Van Lehn, K. (1983). *Felicity conditions in human skill acquisition: Validating an AI-based theory* (Tech. Rep. CIS-21). Palo Alto, CA: Xerox Research Center.

Vergnaud, G. (1982). A classification of cognitive tasks and operations of thought involved in addition and subtraction problems. In T. P. Carpenter, J. M. Moser, & T. A. Romberg (Eds.), *Addition and subtraction: A cognitive perspective* (pp. 39-59). Hillsdale, NJ: Lawrence Erlbaum.

Winograd, T., & Flores, F. (1986). *Understanding computers and cognition: A new foundation for design.* Norwood, NJ: Ablex.

Young, R. M., & O'Shea, T. (1981). Errors in children's subtraction. *Cognitive Science, 6,* 153-178.

Zuboff, S. (1988). *In the age of the smart machine.* New York: Basic.

6 A VIEW FROM PHYSICS

Klaus Schultz
Jack Lochhead
University of Massachusetts

INTRODUCTION

Of the many possible perspectives on physics problem solving, one that has received so much attention from researchers that it can justifiably be called fashionable makes use of comparisons of experts and novices in problem-solving situations. By definition, experts "know how" to solve problems, but what exactly is it that they know? Can we name it, bottle it, and sell it? More seriously, from the standpoint of learning and teaching, can we help novices *become* experts more efficiently than by having them spend years (or decades) of apprenticeship with an expert? In the realm of cognitive development, Piaget playfully dismissed this kind of question about speeding-up, referring to it as the "American question." However, here we are referring at least in part to development of skills and habits rather than to cognitive development. Perhaps the question ought to be phrased in this way: Can we help students avoid years of failure in physics problem solving – by some means other than telling them to give up because they don't have the talent? And (to connect with the theme of this volume) if the answer to the previous question is at least a partial "yes," what can we learn in the process that is useful beyond the learning of physics?

Why is Physics Problem Solving So Difficult?

Physics has long had a reputation as a difficult field. Students often refer to physics as the epitome of a "hard" subject and to successful physics majors as the prototypic "brains." To physics experts, however, the field seems easy compared to other subjects. To these experts, physics is not at all vocabulary- or equation-intensive; the number of basic concepts is relatively few. What has traditionally set physics apart is the two-fold emphasis on the synthesis of concepts and on the combining of concepts, relations, and equations. Now teachers in other sciences that were formerly more descriptive and placed greater demands on students for memorization are joining physics faculty in requiring higher-level skills such as synthesis.

Physics teachers like to tell this story: A student comes for help, saying "I understand the concepts. I just can't do the problems." The physicist somewhat smugly replies that it is precisely by solving problems that you show you understand the concepts. Whether or not that statement is completely true, the fact is that the solving of problems is the preferred, almost universal, means of demonstrating mastery of physics.

Experts and Novices

Comparisons of expert and novice problem solving in physics have helped characterize some of the key features of expert behavior. Are these characteristics exportable to other fields, at least to near-neighbor fields? Based on what is presently known, the question seems difficult to answer in general terms. In this chapter we wish to propose at least four skills frequently observed among physics experts which seem to have broad applicability to a variety of fields. However, the transfer to other fields may require a more deliberate and conscious awareness of the use of these skills than normally accompanies the acquisition of expertise in physics.

Before describing the skills, we will give brief descriptions of "novices" and "experts" for the purposes of this chapter. Novices are not blank slates; we should assume that they have at least been "exposed to" (borrowing a term from medicine) the laws, concepts, and definitions relevant to a given problem space. Experts are knowledgeable in the general domain in question (in this case physics), but are not so familiar with specific problems that they can solve them from memory or by application of a remembered algorithm.

PHYSICS PROBLEMS AND GENERAL PROBLEM SOLVING

The four competencies that we are postulating as candidates for generalized expert problem-solving skills are:

1. the ability to organize quantitative calculations through an understanding of qualitative relations,

2. the ability to represent a problem situation via diagrams or drawings,
3. the ability to organize one's knowledge according to principles that bear on the solution of the problem at hand, and
4. the ability to evaluate the validity of a provisional physical (or other) model through an analogy or chain of analogies.

Each of these competencies will be discussed in turn, with an illustration. Note that none of them contains the word "physics;" none appears to be implicitly physics-connected. Also, none of the competencies is new. The third one, for example, is closely related to the notion of chunking. The first competency was neatly summarized by Champagne, Gunstone, and Klopfer (1983), in a study of expert and novice behaviors, with the diagram of Figure 1.

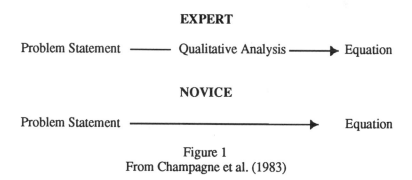

EXPERT

Problem Statement ———— Qualitative Analysis ⟶ Equation

NOVICE

Problem Statement ⟶ Equation

Figure 1
From Champagne et al. (1983)

From Qualitative to Quantitative

How might the expert-novice difference appear in a problem-solving situation? Imagine a problem like this: One is about to cut down a 100-foot tall telephone pole and wants to know how fast it will be moving when it hits the ground. A typical novice might search in his or her memory for potentially relevant equations and focus on those equations that contain a good match between the symbols in the equations, the givens, and the unknowns of the problem statement – what is called means-ends analysis. Perhaps after some floundering with equations of linear motion (e.g., F=ma), the novice might recognize that this is a problem involving rotational motion. What might then come to mind is the rotational analog of F = ma, i.e., the equation linking torque and angular acceleration (see Figure 2). This equation looks simple, but even a novice soon becomes aware of an impasse: The torque varies with the angular position as the pole falls to the ground. The equation describing the motion turns out to be a second-order differential equation with variable coefficients, a very difficult equation to solve analytically. Our typical novice might well give up at the mere thought of such an equation, or perhaps give it the "old college try" before giving up. A "better" novice (an "emerging expert?"), knowing that introductory physics problems never call for such hard mathematics, might realize that there must be a more straightforward approach and eventually arrive at one of the equations expressing the principle of conservation of energy.

FALLING TELEPHONE POLE PROBLEM

Novice's procedure:

Select equation of motion: $\tau = I\alpha$
    (t = torque; a = angular acceleration; I = moment of inertia)
        $\tau = I \, d^2\theta/d \, \tau^2$
But τ varies with θ. So above equation is difficult to solve.

Expert's procedure:

For a pole of length L.

Conservation of energy:
    initial potential energy = final kinetic energy

    $mgh = (1/2)mgL \sim (1/2)mv^2$ (rough approx.)

More precisely:
    Kinetic energy = translational energy of center of mass + rotational energy about center of mass

        $= (1/2)mv^2 + (1/2)I\omega^2$

(v = velocity of center of mass; ω = angular velocity of pole = v/(1/2)L;)
I = moment of inertia about the center of mass.

    $(1/2)mgL = (1/2)mv^2 + (1/2)I \cdot 4v^2 / L^2$

Look up or calculate: $I = mL^2/12$

A bit of algebra:
    $mgL = (4/3)mv^2$

    $v = \sqrt{3gL/4}$

Figure 2

By contrast, an expert would likely start with a qualitative approach, recognizing that the potential energy convertible to kinetic energy is the same as if the entire mass of the pole were concentrated at its center, 50 feet above ground. A first approximation would then lead to the equation $mgh = 1/2 \, mv^2$ (with h = L/2), which can be easily solved for v (the velocity of the center of mass) to give v = gL. (Other parts of the pole would be moving at speeds greater or smaller than this, depending on their location relative to the pivot point at the bottom of the pole.)

However, the kinetic energy of the telephone pole consists of both translational energy (the motion of the center of mass) and rotational energy (around the center of mass). The exact calculations, taking into account the moment of inertia, involve equations that a novice could pull up from memory, if he or she had an efficient way to pull them up. By contrast, an expert, before calling up and sequencing the relevant equations, would likely make a mental note that v will be less than $\sqrt{gL}$ because the initially-available potential energy must be shared between translational and rotational kinetic energies.

So far the expert has been using general problem-solving skills: Start with a simpler situation to get an approximate solution, then consider how the full solution would differ; postpone using numbers and writing down equations. A physics expert would also make use of domain-specific knowledge such as recalling that in such situations the rotational energy is usually of the same order of magnitude as the translational. Consequently the exact value of v is expected to be less than $\sqrt{gL}$ by no more than about a factor 2 (in fact, no more than a factor $\sqrt{2}$, because of the quadratic relation between energy and speed; this latter fact stems from general mathematical sophistication rather than physics knowledge). The calculation outlined in Figure 2 yields v = $\sqrt{3gL/4}$, which differs from $\sqrt{gL}$ by only 13%.

This example, so typical of physics textbook problems, points up a general characteristic of these problems: They are devoid of any real-life connections. The non-physicist reader might well ask why there is any interest at all in this problem, other than the general proclivity of members of all professions to torment their apprentices. As one answer, we could come up with this scenario: Suppose you want to produce a television commercial for a certain kind of pickup truck, to show how tough it is. Before you drop the telephone pole on top of it, you may want to estimate the likely damage in order to see whether the pickup will survive well enough to warrant filming the commercial or whether you need to fake the sequence. So you need to know how fast the pole is falling when it hits the truck. (Of course, in real life the top of the truck is a few feet up from ground level, but that results in only a small change you can easily make once you know how to solve the problem.)

Use of Diagrams

Before writing down *any* equations a physics expert would almost surely make use of a hand-drawn diagram to help identify the relevant principles – very possibly more than one diagram (see Figure 3, related to the above problem). The ability, and even more the willingness, to draw and use schematic diagrams is characteristic of almost all physicists. It is lamentably absent in most novices. To be effective aids in visualization and problem solving, such diagrams can be hand drawn and need not be accurately to scale. Many physicists actually prefer drawings that are not metrically accurate to help them focus on the general principles and avoid spurious results due to special cases or fortuitous choices of parameters.

There are indications that drawing diagrams can be helpful in other sciences and in mathematics as well. Simon (1985) reports that novices (college remedial mathematics students) can be taught to use diagrams, and that this improves their performance on subsequent problems.

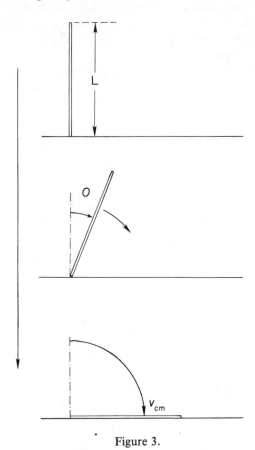

Figure 3.

Selection of Appropriate Principles

For experts to perform as described on the telephone-pole problem, they need what Champagne et al. (1983) call a "comprehensive and integrated motion-of-object schema." One characteristic of such a schema is that it has a hierarchical structure. Mestre, Dufresne, Gerace, Hardiman, & Touger (1988) illustrate how such a structure can be used to teach students to categorize physics problems for the purpose of identifying effective solution paths. Their Hierarchical Analyzer is designed to lead students through a sequence of questions that help them to focus on the relevant physical principles, rather than to immediately try to "write down the equations." As an example of how this computer-based system works, consider a problem which would be recognized by experts as related to the telephone-pole problem although the "cover story" is very different: An object is sliding down a slope of varying pitch, with negligible sliding friction (Figure 4). A "real-life" example might be a skier on a downhill slope. If the height of the ski slope is 100 meters, what is the skier's speed at the bottom? The Hierarchical Analyzer asks the learner a series of multiple-choice questions concerning the physics principles involved in the problem, guiding him or her to an appropriate solution strategy. (See Figure 5. In actual use each question is displayed on screen only after the previous one has been answered correctly.) A great deal of anecdotal evidence suggests that experts go through a similar sequence of self-posed questions, even if very quickly and in some cases unconsciously, to identify the principles and equations best suited to a solution to the problem.

Figure 5. Hierarchical Analyzer Menus & Choices

1
Which principle applies to this part of the problem resolution?
1. Newton's Second Law of Kinematics
2. Angular Momentum
3. Linear Momentum
4. Work and Energy

Please enter your selection: [4]

(B)ackup (M)ain menu (G)lossary (Q)uit (L)ist selections

2
Describe the system in terms of its mechanical energy
1. Conservative system (conservation of energy)
2. Non-Conservative system (work-energy exchange)

Please enter your selection: [1]

(B)ackup (M)ain menu (G)lossary (Q)uit (L)ist selections

3
Describe the changes in mechanical energy. Consider only the energy of one body at some initial and final state
1. Change in kinetic energy
2. Change in potential energy
3. Change in potential and kinetic energies

Please enter your selection: [3]

(B)ackup (M)ain menu (G)lossary (Q)uit (L)ist selections

4
Describe the changes in kinetic energy
1. Change in translational kinetic energy
2. Change in rotational kinetic energy
3. Change in translational and rotational kinetic energies

Please enter your selection: [1]

(B)ackup (M)ain menu (G)lossary (Q)uit (L)ist selections

5
Describe the boundary conditions
1. No initial translational kinetic energy
2. No final translational kinetic energy
3. Initial and final translational kinetic energies

Please enter your selection: [1]

(B)ackup (M)ain menu (G)lossary (Q)uit (L)ist selections

6
Describe the changes in potential energy
1. Changes in gravitational potential energy
2. Changes in spring potential energy
3. Changes in gravitational and spring potential energies

Please enter your selection: [1]

(B)ackup (M)ain menu (G)lossary (Q)uit (L)ist selections

7
Describe the boundary conditions
1. No initial gravitational potential energy
2. No final gravitational energy
3. Initial and final gravitational energy

Please enter your selection: [2]

(B)ackup (M)ain menu (G)lossary (Q)uit (L)ist selections

8
Is there another body in the system which has not been examined?
1. Yes
2. No

Please enter your selection: [2]

(B)ackup (M)ain menu (G)lossary (Q)uit (L)ist selections

9
The Energy Principle states that the work done on the system by all non-conservative forces is equal to the change in the mechanical energy of the system:

$$W_{nf} = E_f - E_i$$

According to your selections,

W = 0 (Conservative system: mechanical energy conserved)

$$E_f = (\tfrac{1}{2}Mv^2)_{1f}$$

$$E_i = (Mgy)_{1i}$$

Please press any key to continue

10
*** Work and Energy ***
1. Problem solved
2. Return to Main Menu to continue solution
3. Review previous solution screens

Please enter your selection:

aSource: J. Mestre, R. Dufresne, W. Gerace, P. Hardiman, & J. Touger, *Promoting expert-like behavior among beginning physics students* (Technical Report No. 178), © 1988, University of Massachusetts, Scientific Reasoning Research Institute, Department of Physics and Astronomy, Amherst, MA. Reprinted with permission

By contrast, left to their own devices, novice students tend to drag up from memory unorganized "laundry lists" of physics terms, problem types, and variable names. They then try to match items from those lists to superficial aspects of the problem statement, and use these superficial matches to select equations they hope will provide a problem solution.

The idea of a tutor helping students see the structure of a knowledge domain holds a great deal of promise. At its present stage of development, the Hierarchical Analyzer has a limited range of responses. However, such a system could be augmented to take into account common misconceptions or specific learner responses, and dispense advice accordingly. Such work is, in fact, being planned (W. Gerace, personal communication, 1989).

Inherent in the hierarchical structure is a set of physics concepts (e.g., energy, momentum, force) which serve to organize physical situations into categories with well-defined solution strategies. In the history of science, each of the physical concepts (e.g., energy) was constructed, and its definition refined over decades and even centuries to make description and solution of problems as simple as possible. The resulting system of concepts is redundant in ways that are useful. (Redundancy is frequently useful in problem-solving and information-processing situations. Examples include language communication and mechanisms of depth perception.) In the example of the falling telephone pole, it is possible to apply either energy or force-and-torque considerations, but one view leads to a much simpler solution path than the other. Expertise is intimately connected with the ability to cast a problem in terms of those concepts that make it relatively simple to solve.

Chains of Analogies

Among experts, the process of selecting a convenient representation (choosing the most advantageous conceptual perspective) may proceed via analogies to previously-solved problems or to situations where the expert feels confident. Novices do not generally make use of such a strategy. For example, most novices are stumped by the question of how much force a table applies to an object resting on top of it; usually they don't believe that there is any such force. This belief persists despite the students' "knowing" (and happily reciting on request) a verbal statement of Newton's Third Law, the general principle that applies to this situation. Even when such contradictions are pointed out to them by an instructor, novices can be exceedingly creative in attempts to evade such contradictions by convoluted ad hoc arguments. To be sure, viewed from an energy perspective, one is apt not to see a need for such a force, since there are no perceptible changes in energy. The need for an upward force exerted by the table can be made more plausible by recourse to an atomic model of solid matter with spring-like forces between neighboring atoms – in effect viewing the table surface as a compressible spring or as a network of springs. For most novices the analogy from solid table to network of springs

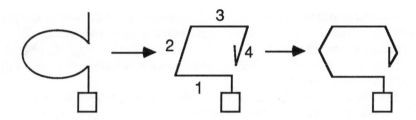

S: Darn it, darn it, darn it . . . What could the circularity [in contrast to the straight rod] do? Why should it matter? How would it change the way the force is transmitted from increment to increment of the spring? Aha. Now let me think about - aha. Now this is interesting. I imagined - I recalled my idea of the square spring and the square is sort of like a circle and I wonder . . . what if I start with a rod and bend it once (places hands at each end of rod in drawing and motions as if trying to bend a rod) and then I bend it again. What if I produce a series of successive approximations to the circle by producing a series of polygons? . . . Clearly there can't be a hell of a lot of difference between the circle and say, a hexagon . . . (Draws hexagonal coil in Figure 4a). Now that's interesting. Just looking at this [hexagon] it occurs to me that when force is applied here, you not only get a bend on this segment, but because there's a pivot here (points to X in Figure 4a), you get a torsion effect . . . Aha! Maybe the behavior of the spring has something to do with twist forces (moves hands as if twisting an object) as well as bend forces (moves hands as if bending an object). That's a real interesting idea . . . That might be the key difference between this [bending rod] which involves no torsion forces, and this [hexagon].

Figure 6.
Source: J. Clement (in press), "Observed methods for generating analogies in scientific problem solving" *Cognitive Science*.

requires too great a conceptual leap. They may accept it from the voice of authority, and may even parrot it back, but it does not make much sense to them.

Clement (in press) has shown how experts spontaneously use chains of analogies to expand their understanding of novel situations. Figure 6 contains segments of one expert's attempts to do this. The problem concerns the force exerted by a stretched helical spring, and more specifically, the comparison of forces exerted by two helical springs that are similar in all respects except their diameters. (Helical springs are the kind used in everyday applications; they are made of wire wound in the shape of a helix.) In the protocol excerpted in Figure 6, the subject attempts to understand the working of helical springs by constructing analogies to square and hexagonal springs, in which the geometrical factors are easier to deal with.

It appears that this strategy of generating, evaluating, and chaining analogies can be used to help novices gain a deeper understanding of technical concepts in physics. Clement (1987), Brown and Clement (1987), and Schultz, Murray, Clement, & Brown (1987) have demonstrated in one-on-one tutoring (both human and computer-based) and in classroom situations that a network of analogies can be used to help students understand the nature and origin of forces exerted by "rigid" stationary bodies such as tables (the same problem as in the first paragraph of this section). Figure 7 displays in iconic form a subset of the network of problem situations used with a particular student or class. The "target" problem, book on the table, is shown in Figure 7. An "anchor" situation (a person's hand pushing on a spring), for which almost all novices have a correct intuition, is shown at the left. Experts know the two situations to be analogous, but novices don't see it; the conceptual gulf is too great. The intermediate situations shown in iconic form in Figure 7 represent other analogous situations that have been found to help students "bridge" the conceptual gap between anchor and target.

The full network contains many more examples. In a specific situation, a skilled teacher or tutor selects and sequences examples from the network to produce a chain of analogies. (The icons at the top and bottom right refer to auxiliary strategies used, including the introduction of mental models and experimental demonstrations.)

Self-Monitoring

In addition to the above four aspects of expertise which are prominent in the literature of problem solving in physics, there is a fifth, more general but probably more critical. None of the four techniques outlined above is guaranteed to yield a correct solution to a given problem. Rather they are heuristics, suggesting promising paths while at the same time guarding against a gross error. While using them, the expert continuously monitors and questions his or her reasoning. One key to expert scientific behavior is this kind of "provisionalism," which results in a

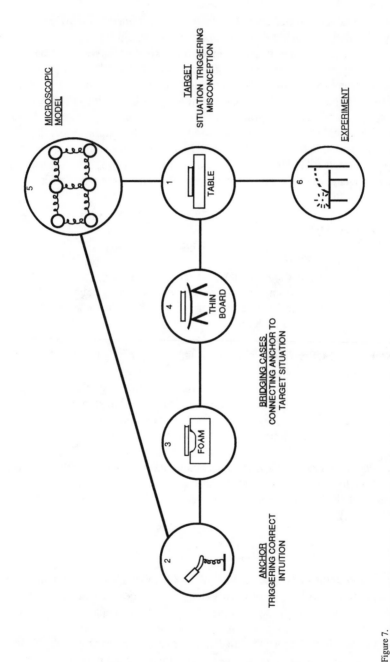

Figure 7.
Source: J. Clement, 1987, Overcoming student's misconceptions in physics: The role of anchoring intuitions and analogical validity. *Proceedings of the Second International Seminar on Misconceptions and Educational Strategies in Science and Mathematics,* (Vol. 3). Cornell University, Ithaca, NY. Reprinted with permission.

constant search for other perspectives that may support or disconfirm previous ones. This is not the same as the common imperative "check your answer." Important as it may be, the latter guards only against mechanical slip-ups, while the former aims to insure against mistakes due to inappropriate points of view.

PROBLEMS IN THE PROBLEM-SOLVING MICROWORLD

Expertise, but Expertise in What?

There is a legitimate question as to the meaning of much research in expert-novice differences. The question is this: Can you say anything about expert-novice differences when the problems posed to experts and novices do not come close to challenging the experts' abilities? The great majority of studies use problems which for the expert are trivial. You do not see real problem-solving, but a kind of tutorial mode (mostly on autopilot), the result of years of explaining this kind of problem to uncomprehending students. To see what the differences in problem-solving procedure are between experts and novices, one must present problems to experts which for them are as novel and as difficult as the problems presented to novices are to them.

The research by Clement (in press) on experts' handling of the "Springs Problem" (Figure 6) is a rare example of research that avoids this shortcoming. In the physics curriculum springs are treated as idealized components of mechanical systems which obey a simple rule (Hooke's Law) relating the force exerted to the amount of stretch or compression. Hooke's Law is asserted but not related to the physical properties of real springs. In the classroom, springs are assumed to be ideal and are described by a single parameter, the "spring constant." When a problem involving springs is stated in terms of other parameters (as is the case in the problem to which Figure 6 refers), the stored knowledge of physicists is not directly applicable. Here the expert must rely on true problem-solving skills rather than semiautomatic routines. It is in situations such as the above that one can observe what expert problem solvers do that is qualitatively different from the behavior of novices.

So-Called Physics Problems

Not only are the problems presented to experts frequently inappropriate, but so are the ones posed to novices. They are not problems in physics, but problems in physics education. They are the products of certain conventions, having more in common with crossword puzzles than with physics. Students can safely assume that, even if there is more than one possible solution path, there is only one correct solution; that all the necessary information to arrive at the solution is provided - no less and no more; that knowledge of the real world is unnecessary, and that relying on it may even be counterproductive. Most students do not object to problems of this kind. On the contrary, they find a certain degree of comfort in dealing with a universe of puzzles, in "psyching out" a set of arbitrary rules.

Some years ago, one of us (K.S.), in an attempt to break out of this state of affairs, presented students with this problem: You are on a one-ton raft in the Mekong River, carrying a load of Jeep tires on deck. You are caught in a crossfire between Viet Cong and government troops firing at each other across your deck. You need to get out of there fast, but in your haste you stall the engine and flood it. You have to use some other way to get moving. Since your neck is at stake, the tires are expendable. By tossing them off the stern, you can propel the boat forward. How far can you move in 30 seconds?

This problem requires several kinds of estimation and decisions about what effects can be neglected if one wants a numerical answer. Writing down and solving the equations is relatively straightforward. The students were told that any halfway reasonable estimates of the necessary parameters would be acceptable, but they were most reluctant to commit themselves by producing quantities from their own heads. They even claimed not to have any idea of the weight of a tire!

Our own experience is that the form (not the content!) of the above example is much closer to what scientists encounter in their work than are the problems one finds at the end of every chapter of almost every physics book. Furthermore, as has been pointed out by Leyden (1984), for the majority of students in science courses the main goal is not training for more advanced courses but preparation for a life as literate adults who act rationally and intelligently. For this majority of students (and also for the minority who become scientists) the expert behavior we should aim to develop is the ability to deal with realistic problems and to mesh information provided in the problem statement with knowledge of the natural environment, rather than the solution of concocted puzzles. Hermetically sealed worlds with arbitrary rules have a place in learning and problem solving, as Papert (1980) has persuasively argued in proposing the notion of "microworlds." However, when the object is to teach students to solve real problems in physics, the role of such artificial worlds is limited.

TRANSFER

Expert knowledge appears to consist of a complex network of multiply inter-connected concepts, organized so that there may be many paths to correct conclusions. Expertise is the ability to reach conclusions with confidence, while constantly on the lookout for the possibility of error. Experts in any given area are often reluctant to apply their skills to another area in which they have little experience. Experience is the yardstick by which experts try to determine the degree of confidence they have in their conclusions.

Transfer, as it is traditionally described, requires a willingness as well as the ability to operate in areas where one has little experience. The wise expert recognizes that this lack of experience imposes a major handicap, but there is a big difference between having the ability to operate as an expert on the one hand and possessing a kind of reflective knowledge of one's repertoire of strategies on the other. In the latter case, it is possible to deliberately apply the strategies to novel situations, keeping in mind that without extensive experience one's judgment will be hampered. Creative leaps, however, do not require this kind of judgment, and may in fact be hindered by it. There are examples in the history of science (such as Einstein's original work leading to special relativity) where great creative advances were made even though (or perhaps because) the scientist did not "know too much" in the domain.

Well short of work at the creative level of Einstein's work, one can still ask whether the problem-solving skills of expert physicists are potentially useful in other domains. One way to answer this question is to point to the physicists who have made great contributions in other fields. A second question is whether some of the skills of physicists can usefully be taught to novices (in physics and in other fields) to help these novices become good problem solvers. Based on the evidence from the examples described in this chapter, we would answer "yes," with the proviso that such teaching must be accompanied by training in systematic self-reflection on one's thinking and problem solving. We have offered several generalizable abilities, along with examples of ways to teach them. We hope these will point a way toward the construction of a unified theory.

REFERENCES

Brown, D., & Clement, J. (1987, April). *Overcoming misconceptions in mechanics: a comparison of two example-based teaching strategies.* Paper presented at the annual meeting of the American Educational Research Association, Washington, DC.

Champagne, A., Gunstone, R., & Klopfer, L. (1983, May). *A perspective on the differences between expert and novice performance in solving physics problems.* Paper presented at the meeting of the Australian Science Education Research Association, Sydney, Australia.

Clement, J. (1987). Overcoming students' misconceptions in physics: The role of anchoring intuitions and analogical validity. *Proceedings of the Second International Seminar on Misconceptions and Educational Strategies in Science and Mathematics,* (Vol. 3, pp. 84-97). Ithaca, NY: Cornell University.

Clement, J. (in press). Observed methods for generating analogies in scientific problem solving. *Cognitive Science.*

Leyden, M.G. (1984). You graduate more criminals than scientists. *The Science Teacher, 51*(3), 26-30.

Mestre, J., Dufresne, R., Gerace, W., Hardiman, P., & Touger, J. (1988). *Promoting expert-like behavior among beginning physics students* (Technical Report No. 178). Amherst, MA: University of Massachusetts, Scientific Reasoning Research Institute, Department of Physics and Astronomy.

Papert, S. (1980). *Mindstorms: Children, computers, and powerful ideas*. New York: Basic.

Simon, M.A. (1985). Diagram drawing: Effect on the conceptual focus of novice problem solvers. In Damarin, S. & Shelton, M. (Eds.), *Proceedings of the Seventh Annual Meeting of the International Group for the Psychology of Mathematics Education, North American Chapter* (pp. 269-273). Columbus, OH: Ohio State University.

Schultz, K., Murray, T., Clement, J., & Brown, D. (1987). Overcoming misconceptions with a computer-based tutor. *Proceedings of the Second International Seminar on Misconceptions and Educational Strategies in Science and Mathematics*, (Vol. 3, pp. 434-447). Ithaca, NY: Cornell University.

7 A VIEW FROM TROUBLE-SHOOTING

Ray S. Perez
U.S. Army Research Institute

The purpose of this chapter is to present a critical review and analysis of the research on troubleshooting. The objectives of this review are to provide a description of the nature of problem-solving skills, knowledges, and abilities that are integral to electromechanical troubleshooting; to describe the types of training programs that have been found to facilitate the development of troubleshooting skills/problem-solving skills; and to describe recent research in cognitive science and artificial intelligence on the teaching of troubleshooting and problem-solving skills that are sufficiently robust to potentially enhance transfer to other tasks/ domains.

Troubleshooting as a Task/Domain

Troubleshooting can best be described as a task distinguishing this chapter from the other chapters in this book which deal with problem-solving skills that are specific to a domain (e.g., computer programming, biology, and medicine). In simple terms, the task of troubleshooting is to locate the problem (malfunction) in a system that is not working properly and then to repair or replace the faulty part (component). The level of specificity at which the troubleshooter must identify the source of the malfunction depends on his or her role and on the demand characteristics of the troubleshooting situation, e.g., the complexity of the system, the time available to the technician, and the nature of the malfunction. The person performing the troubleshooting task may be asked to replace a component or module or to perform some compensatory action that would enable the system to continue to work temporarily.

Which problem-solving skills, knowledges, and abilities are required in any particular instance is dependent in part on what the troubleshooter is expected to do and on the nature of the system he or she is troubleshooting. For example if repair of the system is required, then the troubleshooter must have the necessary knowledges, skills, and abilities to repair or replace the malfunctioning system component. Successful completion of this task will depend on the actions required and on various abilities. During a replace/repair task the troubleshooter may be asked to identify components, use hand tools appropriately, and/or perform relatively simple actions such as replacing a faulty carburetor. The repair and replacement of the components of a system is largely system-specific and requires relatively simple system knowledge, few skills, and minimal ability.

The skills required for the replace/repair task are few and can be rather generic to the extent that the systems that the troubleshooter is asked to repair are similar with respect to components and require the same tools. It is possible in fact that an individual could successfully troubleshoot and repair a system by simply replacing the components of the system until the system worked properly. If the system malfunction involves an adjustment problem rather than a defective component, however, this approach to repairing the system would not work. In fact a review of maintenance effectiveness conducted by the Department of Defense found that nonfaulty components were replaced in 4 to 43 percent of all corrective maintenance actions (Orlanksy & String, 1981).

It is therefore critical that a troubleshooter have the ability to perform diagnostic tests in order to eliminate components from consideration for replacement and to avoid costly replacement of nonfaulty parts. The ability to perform such tests includes several important features, including correct identification and selection of tests that would supply the needed information, identification and access of test points, selection and use of test equipment, interpretation of test results (e.g., the part is faulty or not), and the ability to draw appropriate inferences from the results of the tests (e.g., the reading is within normal limits or not). The ability to perform these tests, much like the ability to repair or replace parts, is mostly system-specific. The location of the tests points may be unique to the system, and the ability to make a determination of whether or not a reading is acceptable requires an appropriate knowledge of normal limits of that parameter for that system. The extent to which the ability to perform tests is generic is dependent on the similarity of test equipment that can be applied to the various systems (e.g., the use of an oscilloscope in electronic troubleshooting).

Using A Troubleshooting Strategy

Another important facet of successful troubleshooting is that the individual search for the source of the problem, in a systematic way. Selecting an appropriate search strategy is one of the most important aspects of troubleshooting expertise (Tenney & Kurland, 1988). Strategies used in troubleshooting vary from simply starting with the component nearest the troubleshooter and tracing back to the source of the problem to generating hypotheses based on an identification of the symptoms of malfunction and a knowledge of how the system functions normally, followed by identifying tests to confirm, reject, and/or revise the hypotheses. Expert troubleshooters often also develop and employ heuristics (i.e., rules of thumb that are useful for solving problems) such as adopting a split-half or bracketing approach or following a predetermined set of procedures. It is these troubleshooting strategies that intuitively appear to have the most promise as generic problem-solving skills.

The importance of these three general abilities—repair and replacement of components, performance of diagnostic tests, and use of a general strategy—has been observed in numerous studies of the differences between good and poor troubleshooters (e.g., Baldwin, 1978; Glaser & Phillips, 1954; Highland, Newman & Waller, 1956; McDonald, Waldrop, & White, 1983; Moore, Saltz, & Hoehn, 1955; Saltz & Moore, 1953; and Saupe, 1954). Morris & Rouse (1985) have summarized the literature on troubleshooting as follows:

> With respect to repair and replacement of components, ineffective troubleshooters demonstrated a lack of elementary knowledge and were poor in executing and verifying the results of their work. When performing tests, poor troubleshooters made fewer tests and more useless tests and were more inconsistent in their consideration of test difficulty. The strategic behavior of poor troubleshooters was characterized by incomplete and inappropriate use of information, ineffective hypothesis generation and testing, and generally less strategic flexibility. (p. 505)

If we accept the thesis that the ability to troubleshoot is comprised of these three abilities, then a training program designed to develop expert troubleshooters must provide training that would teach trainees (novices) to develop skills in all three areas. The training of repair and replace procedures and test performance appears to be rather straightforward. However, the training of elementary knowledge, the appropriate use of test information, effective hypothesis generation, strategic flexibility and the use of strategies for trouble-shooting is much more complex.

Before one can design a training program to teach these skills, one must address the following questions: Should people be trained to employ a particular strategy? If so, what is the prerequisite knowledge needed for the efficient use of strategies in troubleshooting? How do experts develop the ability to use troubleshooting strategies? Can novice troubleshooters be taught when and how to use these strategies? What is the best way to teach a given strategy? Can we train for the transfer of these strategies? In the following sections we will address some of these questions.

What Knowledge is Prerequisite?

A critical question that must be addressed before designing a training strategy is "What knowledge is prerequisite to the efficient use of strategies in troubleshooting?" At a minimal level the troubleshooter must have some knowledge of the system and of troubleshooting algorithms or procedures.

With regard to the prerequisite knowledge needed to be an effective troubleshooter, Anderson (1983) has suggested that experts acquire two types of knowledge: declarative knowledge (facts, concepts, rules, and principles) and procedural knowledge (step–by–step). In this formulation the acquisition of declarative knowledge gives rise to procedural knowledge. Within this framework, the teaching of troubleshooting procedures must be preceded by the teaching of the facts, concepts, rules, and principles of how the system/equipment works. Further, the teaching of declarative and procedural knowledge must be done as an integrated whole. Attempts to teach only the theoretical principles of troubleshooting, however, have met with failure. Morris and Rouse (1985) conclude on the basis of their review of research on the effects of training troubleshooting using instruction on theoretical principles that "instruction in theoretical principles is not an effective way to produce good troubleshooters."

The results of such studies of troubleshooting training are consistent with research in other domains such as process control (Brigham & Laios, 1975; Crossman & Cooke, 1974; Morris & Rouse, 1985) and mathematical problem solving (Mayer, Stiehl, & Greeno, 1972). In these studies an instructional focus on the explicit training of fundamentals or principles failed to enhance performance and in some cases even degraded the performance of the trainees. Its appears that the fundamental understanding of theoretical principles, facts, and concepts is necessary for answering theoretical questions, but instruction that does not also develop the ability to apply these fundamentals in concrete situations is not likely to develop successful problem solvers.

The Effects of Practice

Several researchers have investigated the effects of the opportunity for practice as an important variable in acquiring and improving troubleshooting skills (Duncan & Shepherd, 1975; Johnson & Rouse, 1982a, 1982b). These researchers provided opportunities for trainees to practice newly acquired skills on actual equipment or on devices that simulated the equipment. Duncan and Shepherd (1975) compared a form of guided practice with unguided practice on a mock-up of a control room operating panel. Johnson and Rouse (1982a, 1982b) provided practice to automobile engine or aircraft engine trainees in either a context-free or a context-specific environment. These studies demonstrate that practice improves performance, irrespective of the mode of practice (guided or non-guided) or the context.

The Effects of System Complexity on Troubleshooting Performance

The complexity of a system is a function of the number of components in the system, the number of functional relationships among those components, and the number of feedback loops involved. Performance is determined, in large part, not only by the technician's skills, but also by an interaction between system complexity and the amount of time the individual is given to isolate a fault.

Various research studies (Brooke & Duncan,1981; Goldbeck, Bernstein, Hillix, & Marx, 1957; McDonald et al., 1983; Rouse, 1978a, 1979b, 1979c;) have found that troubleshooting performance is degraded by the realism, size, and complexity of the system. Such factors as increasing the realism (e.g., from two dimensional presentations to three), the number of components, the number of functional relationships among those components, and the complexity of the systems components (e.g., complexity of the electronic boards) results in less successful troubleshooting in these systems. Rouse (1979a) also found that the number of functional relationships among the system components is highly correlated with the amount of time subjects required to troubleshoot. McDonald et al., (1983) observed that increases in complexity of actual electronic boards increased the time required and the number probes used to troubleshoot a system. Rouse (1979a) found that fault location performance degrades as the number of system feedback loops increases. Poorer troubleshooting performance is therefore correlated with increasing complexity of systems, increasing the processing demands and overloading the troubleshooter's working memory.

Generation of Hypotheses

Generating a hypothesis as to the cause of a symptom prior to actually troubleshooting the system has also been found to improve performance. Moore et al., (1955) required trainees to list the possible causes (hypotheses) of the failures and identify critical tests of these hypotheses prior to troubleshooting the faulty system. Performance of trainees who performed this exercise was significantly enhanced. Similarly, the ability to organize information in a usable form has been demonstrated to improve performance. Miller (1975) trained radar mechanics to relate instruction in system functioning to the actions they performed while troubleshooting. In this study the proper functioning of the system was presented in terms of casual sequences using schematics of the actual equipment. Students were encouraged to organize and chunk the information they were given by the experimenters. They were trained to chunk the information of symptoms, system behavior, and the actions required to perform appropriate tests. After training, students receiving the experimental treatment were faster in performing checks and adjustments, made fewer errors, and were frequently more successful in troubleshooting.

Summarizing the current state of the knowledge on troubleshooting, Morris and Rouse (1985) suggest

> Either a troubleshooter should be explicitly instructed in how to approach problems or they [sic] should be forced to use their knowledge of the system explicitly in deciding what to do. Unfortunately, a definitive statement as to which of these is the better approach cannot be made because of the lack of data. The latter has not been evaluated in a transfer study, and the two approaches have not been compared with each other experimentally. (p. 527)

In an earlier article Rouse (1985) suggested a further limitation of the procedural approach to training.

> The procedural approach is fundamentally limited by the fact that one can seldom anticipate all of the events or combinations that may occur in a particular system. Thus, the operators and maintainers inevitably encounter an event for which there is no procedure, or a combination of events for which it is not clear which procedure, if any, should be used. In such situations, proceduralized training is of no use. (p. 104)

Moreover, given the non-deterministic nature of the digital electronics that have been introduced into highly sophisticated kinds of equipment, the task of fault isolation becomes even more problematic (Gott & Kieras, 1988); faults cannot be predicted such that it is next to impossible to develop procedures for fault isolation for these systems in advance.

To my knowledge, only two studies to date (Frese, 1989 and Swezey, Perez, & Allen, in press) have reported evaluated training that combines both system knowledge with knowledge of troubleshooting procedures. The latter study was an experiment on the effects of different instructional strategies on troubleshooting performance on a reference task and on a transfer task. The reference task consisted of subjects troubleshooting different faults on a mock-up of a diesel engine on which they had been trained. The transfer task required the trainees to troubleshoot a different piece of equipment. One group received a procedure-based (procedural knowledge) instructional strategy characterized by a step-by-step presentation of the operation of a diesel engine and how to troubleshoot it. A second group was given an instructional strategy based on conceptual information (declarative knowledge) on diesel engine components, their structure and function, and on troubleshooting. Instruction for the third group utilized an integrated procedural and conceptual instructional strategy. Data from this study indicate that subjects receiving the procedural-based instruction performed more accurately, but slower, than did subjects whose training consisted of conceptual (generic system) knowledge on the reference task. On the transfer task, however, the subjects receiving an instructional strategy that included information concerning the structure and function of a system were faster and made fewer errors. The authors concluded that if the goal of training is to train technicians as quickly as possible to troubleshoot a specific system, then only procedural knowledge is needed. However, if the goal of training is to train technicians to maintain a family of similar but different equipment (i.e., automobiles with varying fuel systems), then the training must include both procedural and declarative knowledge in order to ensure the transfer of generic troubleshooting skills.

On the basis of the results of the studies reviewed it would appear that teaching conceptual knowledge is not an effective approach to train troubleshooters. Rather it is teaching people how to use their knowledge in a specific context that leads to effective troubleshooting.

A Cognitive Model of Troubleshooting

Because of the increasing complexity of current and future systems, the strategy of presenting trainees with a fixed set of explicit procedures or heuristics adequate for finding and locating faults in each system is an unrealistic goal. Researchers have therefore looked to alternative ways of training troubleshooters. Many of these alternative training programs are based on information processing models of learning and include sophisticated computer simulations. They focus on the acquisition of knowledge, knowledge structures, and their representations.

Perez and Seidel (1986) have suggested that a cognitive theory of training or learning must be explicit as to the role of the knowledges, skills, processes, and metacognitive strategies required to perform a task. Metacognitive processes are defined as the knowledge and control a troubleshooter has over his or her own thinking and learning activities. According to Perez and Seidel, metacognition includes at least three processes: (1) self-monitoring or awareness of what skills, strategies, and resources are needed to perform a task effectively; (2) self-regulation, to ensure the successful completion of the task; and (3) executive control strategies, to evaluate the effectiveness of strategies and to change strategies as necessary. Examples of these strategies would include checking what information (i.e., schematics) and tests are needed to troubleshoot the malfunctioning system, developing and planning a strategy for isolating the fault, evaluating the effectiveness of the strategy, and testing and revising the strategy or selecting another.

Greeno (1980) has raised a series of critical issues about the nature of what is acquired by trainees during troubleshooting training: What is the organization of the knowledge, the characteristics of the learner's understanding, the knowledge and information processing requirements for solving problems, and the nature of the competences entailed in human performance requiring specific knowledge and skills resulting from long-term learning and extended experiences? In order to address these issues Greeno and Simon (1988) and others have suggested that task analytic techniques and knowledge engineering approaches be utilized to study the performance of experts and novices. This approach has as its focus the study of the parameters of the task performance by experts and has been performed in such varied areas as chess (Simon, 1980); geometry (Greeno, 1977); genetics (Smith & Good, 1984); physics (Larkin & Reif, 1976); economics (Voss, Blaise, Means, Greene, & Ahwesh,1989); avionic troubleshooting (Gitomer, 1988); and electrical and mechanical troubleshooting (White & Frederiksen, 1985, 1986, 1987).

Wiggs and Perez (1988) have outlined how these combined approaches of task analysis, cognitive task analysis, and knowledge acquisition techniques could be used for the design of instruction for training troubleshooting. Glaser and Bassok (1989) have also used this approach to characterize the complexity of school learning in the subject areas of reading, mathematics, science, and social studies.

Research on a Cognitive Model of Troubleshooting

Gitomer (1984) and Glaser et al., (1985) have found evidence for the role of a mental model in the troubleshooting of avionic equipment. The term "mental model" refers to an understanding of a system that includes knowledge of the possible states of each component of the system as well as the temporal and causal links between the components of the system. A mental model is thought to consist of images and to be similar to a computer model that is "runnable." A mental model can be used by an expert technician, and there is evidence (Smith & Spoehr, 1985; Kurland & Tenney, 1988) that experts do use these models by allowing the model to mentally "run," observing the effects that a change in one component of the system has on the other components of the system.

Similarly, Mayer (1977) has demonstrated in learning a computer language that providing students with a conceptual model of the language facilitates the acquisition of that language. Kieras and Bovair (1984) have further shown that providing students with instruction on the "structure and functioning" of a system prior to their receiving information on "how to use" that system produces faster learning and fewer errors in the operation of that system. Smith and Spoehr (1985) demonstrated that teaching students a model of a complex system increased their recall of the components of the system, their understanding of the procedural steps involved in the operation of the system, and the accuracy with which they carried out these steps. This training also enhanced learner reasoning about a new procedure for localizing a fault.

Tenney and Kurland (1988) studied the acquisition of troubleshooting expertise in radar mechanics in the U.S. Army. In this study radar technicians who had one, five, or ten years of experience on the job were interviewed. Interview protocols were analyzed in terms of four variables that had been found in earlier studies to differentiate experts from novices: depiction of physical features (e.g., panels, meters, lights), depiction of current voltage, depiction of information flow (one-way), and depiction of information flow (in loops). Tenney and Kurland observed the following differences between the experts and novices on these variables: (a) Novices appeared to focus on the physical or surface aspects of the radar system, whereas the experts focused on the functional aspects of the radar system; (b) Novices tended to think of the flow of information in a serial manner, rather than in a number of feedback loops as did the experts; (c) Novices focused on how the electrical power is distributed throughout the radar system, whereas experts focused on the flow of information. (An understanding of both the flow of electricity and the flow of information—electrical and/or mechanical—among the components of the system is required in order for a technician to repair a radar system.)

The nature of the representation of the models that experts use to solve problems has been investigated by Forbus and Genter (1986) who suggest that the quantitative mathematical models used by experts are derived from a progression of causal and qualitative models. Forbus and Genter further observed that it is the "tacit knowledge" and "implicit properties" of devices that distinguish experts from novices. The goal of the training systems that will be described in the following sections, therefore, is to attempt to make use of the implicit and tacit knowledge of experts.

The analysis of expert performance and the formulation of an expert performance model of real world problem-solving tasks such as medical diagnosis, electronic troubleshooting, and computer programming have been the subject of considerable research in artificial intelligence and cognitive psychology. An expert performance model is the result of an analysis of the cognitive processes used by the expert to perform a task. This model consists of declarative knowledge (i.e., facts, concepts, and principles), formal rules (i.e., rules regarding how to use these facts), procedural knowledge (i.e., skills), meta-rules (i.e., rules for applying formal and procedural rules), heuristics (i.e., rules of thumb), and relations among all these elements (Hamill, 1984; Hart, 1986). The major difference between troubleshooting and other domains such as computer programming or mathematical problem solving is that in troubleshooting there is greater complexity. In addition to declarative and procedural knowledge, meta-rules, and heuristic requirements, the troubleshooter's performance is largely influenced by his or her knowledge of the system/device to be repaired (Gott,1987; Gott & Pokorny,1987).

Use of a Cognitive Model in Instruction

In this section we describe several approaches to education and training that use various aspects of a cognitive model for training along with related cognitive science constructs and artificial intelligence technologies to develop troubleshooting skills. One such effort is the Navy sponsored SOPHIE Project (SOPHisticated Instructional Environment; Brown & Burton, 1975). Brown and Burton (1986) conceptualized the task of troubleshooting as the ability of the technician to

> pick up a schematic and figure out what would happen if any part were faulted. That is, the student must know what role that part actually plays on the overall functioning of a circuit and what mechanism it exploits to achieve its role in that overall plan. (pp. 79-80)

In their research on how experts troubleshoot, they found that experts construct and use various types of models of the structural characteristics of the device components. According to Brown and Burton, it is the development of these structural models that leads to a functional understanding of the device components. These models are based on implicit assumptions about how the device's components are related to each other within a particular context. As an example, they describe how an expert compares the behavior of a transistor to that of an amplifier or a switch, depending on how the transistor is connected to other components. In other words, the experts develop a metaphor of the function of the device which is used to help understand the device and to reason about the nature of the fault. The metaphor that is used by the expert is, however, "specific to the particular situation or context in ways that are not captured in the models themselves" (Brown & Burton, 1986, p. 68).

An example of the application of these constructs to training is the STEAMER project. STEAMER is a manipulable simulator for training engineers to operate steam propulsion plants aboard large naval ships. The operation of these large steam-propelled ships is extremely complex, and the expertise necessary to operate and maintain them requires years of training. The STEAMER simulation was designed using AI software tools to test Brown and Burton's theory of troubleshooting and to teach trainees the procedures for operating and maintaining a steam plant. The primary goal of STEAMER was not to teach procedural knowledge about the operation of the steam plant but to teach a robust mental model that could be used to reason qualitatively about the steam plant (Holland, Hutchins, McCandless, Rosenstein, & Weitzman, 1987). Brown and Burton felt that the procedures for maintaining the steam plant would evolve from the trainees' "deep" understanding of how the steam plant worked. STEAMER presented trainees with a series of high-level abstractions in the form of graphic images, each depicting the steam plant and its behavior. These depictions of the components of the steam plant were presented in a hierarchical manner with the major plant parameters presented first, followed by more detailed simulations of subsystem components. The simulations of the steam plant were based on mathematical models of the plant's behavior. The graphic interface presented to the trainees a qualitative model of these quantitative models, representing the internal behavior of the plant in a form that could be inspected. These qualitative models presented the trainees with "runnable" models that enabled the trainees to observe the implicit interdependencies and dynamic processes of the system. Although, no data exist to date to support the effectiveness of STEAMER or to verify Brown and Burton's theory of troubleshooting, the architecture of STEAMER has been influential in the AI research community in motivating other research studies and in the construction of other AI-based systems. A sample of these systems and the theory underlying them will be discussed in the following sections.

Device Model

In tasks like medical diagnosis and troubleshooting where a device or system is part of the performance, the mental model held by the physician or technician regarding how a device or system works enables him or her to infer procedures for the operation and repair of that system or device. This mental model can also serve as the basis for the generation of procedural steps when exact procedural steps are forgotten, are not accessible, or are not known. The role of device/system knowledge has been studied in medical diagnosis by Clancey (1986) where the "system" (the human body) has not changed for a least five hundred years. A system model of the body is used by the physician to reason about what is wrong with the patient. The system model used by the doctor for diagnosing a patient's illness consists of his or her knowledge of the facts, relations, and functions of each of the components (organs) of the system. The central concept here is that the doctor who understands how the organs of the human body function and how they are interrelated to each other will be able to use this knowledge to diagnose the cause of the symptoms observed and treat the patient appropriately. An example of this approach is Shortliffe's (1976) MYCIN and NEOMYCIN, expert systems for medical diagnosis which consist of the knowledge compiled in production rules that mimick the diagnostic problem solving of an expert physician.

An Example of A Device Model: GUIDON

An intelligent tutor program is an expert system that emulates a human expert. Most such tutors consist of knowledge compiled into production rules for teaching problem solving. Although MYCIN and NEOMYCIN performed well as expert systems, they were not originally designed as tutors. They are not suitable for teaching the diagnostic process because the reasoning underlying the diagnosis process is not transparent to the student nor is the system designed to emulate the actual reasoning processes used by an expert physician. (See Park, Perez, and Seidel, 1987 for a detailed discussion of the requirements for an intelligent tutor.) The objective of the GUIDON project was to build an intelligent tutor based on expert knowledge (NEOMYCIN, Clancey & Letsinger, 1981) enhanced by a well organized body of knowledge about medical diagnosis and a set of heuristic strategies required for using this knowledge for practical problem solving. Clancey (1986) obtained the expertise for the additional components for GUIDON by eliciting and modeling the explanations from an expert physician-teacher. The resultant knowledge base is organized into categories of general principles that represent domain knowledge, definitions and relations, causal relations, meta-rules, heuristics, and strategies. Thus, Clancy was able to represent the strategies used for diagnosis as a general reasoning process of inferencing that was separate from specific domain knowledge. This reconfiguration of the expert knowledge base allowed Clancy and his students to construct an expert system that is domain-independent, using reasoning strategies underlying a class of problem-solving tasks requiring heuristic classification and a predetermined taxonomy. These general reasoning strategies were then used to match the features of the data to candidate categories (HERACLES, Clancey, 1984). This model (Figure 1) consists of three components: a general model that contains information about the domain, an inferencing procedure (engine) or set of if-then rules that is used to build and draw, then a situation-specific model that contains information specific to a problem. The role of the inferencing engine is to interpret information in the general model and select information to develop the situation-specific model from which a solution or diagnosis is generated.

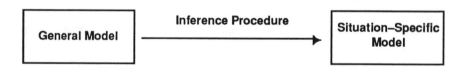

Figure 1.
A problem solving model for diagnostic thinking from "Qualitative Student Models" by
W. J. Clancey, 1986, *Annual Review of Computer Science, 1*, 395.
Copyright 1986 by Annual Reviews Inc., Palo Alto, CA.

The importance of the Clancey model is that it describes the reasoning process in an abstracted way that is domain-independent and emphasizes how problem solvers use their system knowledge (of the physiology, anatomy, etc. of the human body) to develop situation-specific solutions. The importance of the design of the GUIDON system is that it is general enough to be used in other domains such as electronic troubleshooting. In troubleshooting the technician also must recognize malfunctions from their symptoms and must select from a fixed set of methods the one that is most appropriate to the specific situation. The use of heuristics rather that a fixed set of procedures or algorithms is not only important in medical diagnosis but is also germane to troubleshooting in which it is often infeasible to use algorithms because of the uncertainty of the available information about the problem and/or the incompleteness of the technician's general model of the device (e.g., unknown system facts).

Functional Qualitative Model

Clancey (1986) has recently revised the diagnostic model used in MYCIN. This new diagnostic model of thinking separates knowledge from the procedures (production rules) that use that knowledge. This new diagnostic model of thinking has been implemented in Clancey's (1986) GUIDON system. The system consists of a diagnostic model that reasons in an abstracted, domain-independent way, where problem solvers use their general knowledge of the system to formulate situation-specific solutions. This "functional qualitative" diagnostic model consists of three problem-solving components: (a) a general model that contains knowledge about the world of expert medical diagnosis, (b) a situation-specific model that contains information in an abstracted form (from the first component) about the specific problem under consideration, and (c) an inferencing procedure or engine that draws and interprets information germane to the specific situation from the general model to generate a solution or diagnosis.

The evidence that exists to support the effectiveness of GUIDON as a tutor is sparse and consists mainly of informal evaluations. However, Clancey's notions of problem solving have been influential in the design of other tutors.

An Example of A Qualitative Model: QUEST

White and Frederiksen (1986) have also been involved in conducting research on the effects of mental models and qualitative reasoning on electronic troubleshooting. In order to test their ideas about the teaching of troubleshooting they developed a system which they called QUEST (Qualitative Understanding of Electrical System Troubleshooting), a reactive learning environment in which students are presented with a series of electronic circuit problems. The architecture of QUEST consists of a device simulation and the troubleshooting expert (see Figure 3.) QUEST is of interest not only because is it an example of a system designed to use a qualitative model for instructing students in troubleshooting electronic circuits, but also because it incorporates the notion of using a progression of qualitative models as an instructional strategy. The goal of this research project was to build a tutor that would present students with an environment that provides this progression of device models that correspond to increasing levels of expertise and to investigate the effects of experience with this tutor on student ability to troubleshoot electronic circuits.

White and Frederiksen (1986) identify three dimensions along which the qualitative models in their program vary. These dimensions are: perspective, order, and degree of elaboration. QUEST is based on Brown and deKleer's (1985) model of problem solving which equates the knowledge to be acquired by a student for successful problem solving in a specific scientific domain with a mental model of the domain. This model contains as the units of knowledge the concepts and laws of the domain. The model is robust enough to enable the generation of casual explanations and can enable problem solving in varying conditions and contexts.

According to Brown and deKleer, the acquisition of this model enables students to acquire "cognitive adaptiveness"—a prerequisite for problem solving in an nondeterministic domain such as modern digital "black box" electronic systems. White and Frederiksen's goal for teaching trouble-shooting is "the integration of multiple, alternative conceptualizations of circuit operation that enable robust causal reasoning and deep understanding of domain phenomena (p. 42)." The formulation of progressive qualitative models has been accomplished by White and Frederiksen (1986), who analyzed the task domain to identify the top–level goals, strategies, skills, and knowledge of expert performers. The strategies are then further decomposed to identify the prerequisite knowledge needed to teach an understanding of each strategy and to determine the variables that affect and determine the form and use of these strategies. Expertise of troubleshooting is decomposed into simple models that teach only about simple electrical concepts such as voltage or simple troubleshooting strategies such as the split-half technique. These models consist of declarative device knowledge of electrical circuits, procedures for investigating these circuits, and a control structure for making strategic decisions about how the declarative and procedural knowledge will be used to solve a subset of problems appropriate to that specific model. As the student progresses through QUEST each model is more complex than the preceding one, adding additional concepts or methods of reasoning and increasing the difficulty of the problem sets. The student is presented with graphic simulations and causal explanations for circuit behavior that vary in the complexity of information provided in the device model, in the complexity of the problem sets, and in the control structure. Figure 2 illustrates this progression of device model complexity. (Control structure needed for technical problem solving is described by White and Frederiksen, 1987, as "the determination of what goal to pursue next when reasoning about the behavior of a circuit" [p. 13].) The system also enables the student to develop his own runnable models of electric circuits.

The goal of these activities is to enable the student to understand the general principles governing the behavior of electronic circuits, to predict states of components, and to perform a constrained set of troubleshooting operations. QUEST's environment is flexible enough to allow the student to build and modify circuits while still receiving explanations of the states of components.

In summary QUEST provides students with procedural knowledge in the form of sequences of troubleshooting heuristics coordinated with a progression of

Figure 2a.

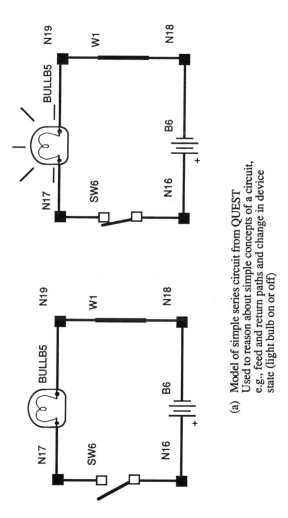

(a) Model of simple series circuit from QUEST
Used to reason about simple concepts of a circuit,
e.g., feed and return paths and change in device
state (light bulb on or off)

Illustration of the device model progression of QUEST, from "Intelligent Tutors as Testers"
by J. R. Frederiksen and B. Y. White (in press),

Figure 2b.

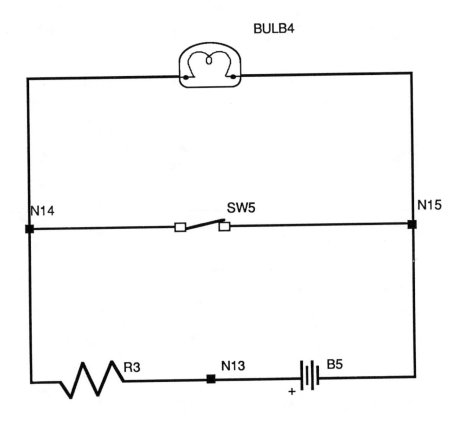

(b) More advanced parallel circuit model from QUEST
New idea is incorporated: light is off because it
has been shorted by the closed switch which is in
parallel to the bulb; purely conductive path has no
voltage drop across it, so light is off.

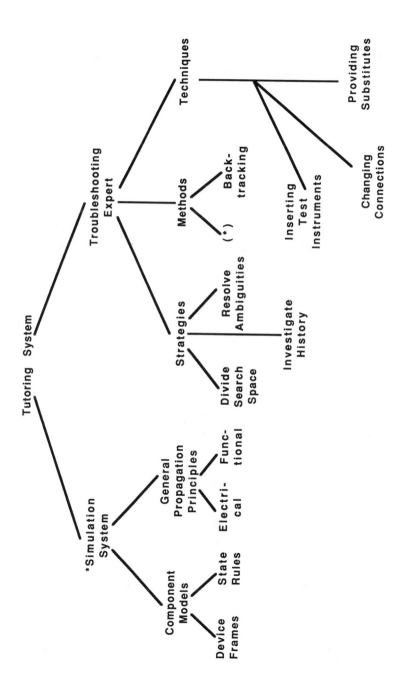

Figure 3. Diagram of QUEST's tutoring system architecture from "Intelligent Tutors as Intelligent Testers" by J. R. Frederiksen and B. Y. White (in press).

models that vary in complexity of the concepts, heuristics, and associated control structures. Each model includes declarative device knowledge (facts, rules, and principles about electronic circuits), procedures for investigating circuits (troubleshooting heuristics), and a control structure (plan for interpreting information) for strategic decisions about the use of the declarative and procedural knowledge. Each model allows exploration of a microworld-like environment by providing the student with a runnable simulation of electronic circuit behavior at a specific level of understanding. While learning is problem-driven, it is also learner-controlled, i.e., students have the freedom to make decisions about conditions under which they want to learn and about the type of problems they want to pursue. White and Frederiksen maintain that this capability of QUEST fosters "learning-to-learn" strategic knowledge and "cognitive adaptiveness" which enables students to transfer these skills to other domains.

Research evidence for the effectiveness of QUEST and support for the theory of teaching troubleshooting it embodies are preliminary. White and Frederiksen (1986) have reported an evaluation study in which seven high schools students who had no previous knowledge of electronic troubleshooting were given six one-hour sessions with QUEST. On the post-test six of the seven students were able to make accurate predictions about circuit behavior and could troubleshoot open circuits and shorts-to-grounds in a group of circuits. The generality of these results is limited by the small number of subjects, by the lack of a control group, and by the fact that the post-test problems were similar to those presented in the treatment session. Based on this study, White and Frederiksen identified several weaknesses of QUEST including the less–than–optimal sequencing of problems, the inadequacy of the depth of explanations, the lack of variety in the problems presented, the lack of a physical model, and finally the lack of flexibility of the troubleshooting heuristics provided. Perhaps the most serious deficiency of QUEST is pointed out by Wenger (1987):

> The central question of integration of multiple conceptualizations, mentioned by White and Frederiksen as a key to deep understanding, is not addressed seriously - in particular the issue of meaning of concepts in electricity in the context of the students' model of the world. This conceptual integration almost inevitably involves an interactive process whereby analogies to existing concepts are tuned and implicit assumptions are exposed. (p. 97)

Another instructional issue for the developers of QUEST is that of how to handle student errors and correct student misconceptions. White and Frederiksen (1986) suggest that discrepancies that exist between the students' mental models and those that we were trying to teach *were not due* to the inevitability of misconceptions, but rather to limitations of the learning environment. The theoretical as well as practical significance of this statement is that it implies that if the limitations of QUEST were corrected, then student misconceptions and errors could be prevented altogether. This sounds much like the claim by Skinner (1968) for "error-less learning." (p. 56)

Further experimentation is needed to isolate the effects of each of the instructional variables that is embedded in the design of QUEST (i.e., the effects on learning and transfer of the the presentation of progressively more complex mental models).

An Example of a Coached Practice Environment: Sherlock

Coaching is a guided-discovery learning environment in which the student controls the instructional activity by modifying the environment. The environment of coaching is usually a game. Games such as "How the West was Won" (Burton & Brown, 1979) and LOGO (Feurzeig, 1968; Papert, 1980) have been selected for coaching because of their conceptual simplicity and intrinsic motivational value. Unlike the tutors discussed earlier, the roles of the automated coach are to serve as an advisor, to make students aware of learning opportunities, and to ensure that they do not get stuck while playing the game. The task of the coach is not to lecture the student but to encourage the learning of specific skills that are built into the game activities. The coach does this by pointing out existing learning opportunities and, more importantly, by transforming the students' failures into learning experiences. This is accomplished by presenting the students with a variety of activities with hints, explanations, and help menus. The coach must also have some method for identifying when students make errors and when they are stuck. The most important instructional design decisions for developers of coaches are questions about how to determine when to interrupt the student, how to correct the student's errors, and what comments are most appropriate at any given point.

The design of LOGO was influenced by the theories of cognitive development of Piaget. LOGO's fundamental goal and basic method of instruction is to use the computer as a tool that the student can manipulate to explore the concepts and principles of geometry. According to Papert (Laird & Newell, 1983), it is more important to help children to learn to develop and debug their own theories than it is to teach them theories we consider correct.

SHERLOCK is a coached-practice environment developed for training avionic troubleshooting. It is a device-based tutor that was built on a cognitively based system for training troubleshooting. The primary goal of the system is to enhance Air Force technicians' procedural investigation of airborne digital electronic devices and their associated test equipment. The simulation of the physical system presented to the technician is only a partial representation of the equipment. SHERLOCK includes pre-specified diagnostic expertise but does not include a runnable device simulation or a dynamic expert diagnostician. The system uses what the authors refer to as a pedagogically robust and well–documented "problem space-graph" as its cognitive model. A problem space is described by Laird and

Newell (1983) as the various operators and steps in a problem solution. Problem space-graphs, then, are used to describe the alternative probable solution paths a technician will pursue during a complex fault–isolation activity. The use of problem space-graphs is based on the assumption that a task can be completely described by descriptions of the problem states and a set of general primitive operators for moving from one state to the next. For example the area of subtraction has been characterized using a problem space-graph by Langley, Wogulis, & Ohlsson (1987). A set of general primitive operators used by students to solve subtraction problems is presented in Figure 4. Figure 5 presents the problem space as a top view of the test equipment used in the maintenance of the F-15 fighter jet.

SHERLOCK uses the problem space-graph method to present the structure of the problem-solving knowledge of a very complex technical domain—troubleshooting of the F-15. It provides concentrated practice opportunities via interactive simulations coupled with a multi-level set of plan-action structures. Focusing on the organization and structure of subject matter content has been proposed by Glaser (1973) as a powerful method for facilitating acquiring knowledge and remembering.

The content of the SHERLOCK tutor was derived using a cognitive representation in the form of a problem space-graph and from two types of analysis. First, a cognitive analysis that compared the performance of skilled and less skilled apprentice technicians on realistic fault isolation tasks was performed (Gitomer, 1984, 1988; Glaser et al., 1985; Gott, Bennett, & Gillet, 1986). Second, knowledge engineering studies using Air Force avionics experts were carried out in which less-skilled technicians were found to lack the necessary problem-solving skills (i.e., a device model or a plan or strategy for investigating a component) to isolate a malfunction. The range of performance by these technicians was represented with a problem space-graph formalism developed by Glaser et al. (1985) adapted from a method used by Newell and Simon (1972). The problem space-graph formalism was used to represent the hierarchies of plans and actions used by most of the technicians in isolating faults. Figure 5 provides an example of these prototypic structures and was the basis for the tutor's domain knowledge. The problem space-graphs represent the top-level view of the equipment used to maintain the F-15— a test station that has the functions of generating, routing, and measuring signals to test system components. Technicians have a limited knowledge of the structure and functions of the system, and they are trained to treat symptom components as "black boxes." When a component is suspected of having a malfunction, the technician tests it and, based on the test station results, removes and replaces it. Figure 6 is the device model representation commonly held by experts in which the test station's functional properties (stimulus generation, stimulus measurement, and stimulus routing or switching) are emphasized.

The primary goal of SHERLOCK is to teach technicians a mental model for an electronic test. SHERLOCK's theory of problem solving/electronic troubleshooting is viewed as "device model-guided plans and actions that are regulated by executive control processes" (Lesgold, Lajoie, Bunzo, & Eggan, in press). In this view the conceptual base for procedural and strategic knowledge is the electronic test. SHERLOCK 's instructional goals are to teach not only the mental model of the test but also a goal structure (plan) for investigating the system components, procedural knowledge in the form of specific fault–isolation actions that instantiate the top-level goal structure, and additional strategic (control) knowledge to inform decision making during problem solving. Therefore, the instructional goals for SHERLOCK are: to develop the technician's mental model of an electronic test on the F-15 aircraft test station, to teach the plans and actions for conducting the tests, and to teach the strategic control processes required to isolate failures that occur during the testing process. SHERLOCK accomplishes these goals by providing 34 troubleshooting scenarios with menus and hints. For each scenario an extensive set of menus is provided to the technician as a group of options from which he can select; they reflect the developers' analysis of the problem-solving process. Hints provided to the technicians are organized along two dimensions: the type of explicitness and the level of explicitness. Type hints are based on the current status of the technician in the testing activity (e.g., what action to take and how to interpret the outcome of the action). The level of explicitness is varied across five degrees of elaboration and directiveness. Explicitness varies from a recapitulation of information presented already to explanations and suggested next steps. Examples of SHERLOCK's menus and hints are presented in Figure 7.

In SHERLOCK the learner is presented with a simulation of the external controls of the equipment rather than its internal behavior. In STEAMER and QUEST the concern was with a simulation that represented the conceptual fidelity of the equipment. In Sherlock the concern is with physical fidelity, representing as closely as possible the physical work environment (i.e., control panels of the test station).

Data regarding of the effectiveness of SHERLOCK were obtained in an experiment (Gott & Kieras, 1989) in which SHERLOCK was evaluated by comparing a control group who received on-the-job informal training against an experimental group who worked about 20 hours on SHERLOCK's 34 problems. Each tutoring session lasted from 2 to 3 hours, with the experimental treatment lasting an average of 12 working days. The experimental group was superior to the control group on posttest measures, including both a "structured, thinking-aloud verbal protocol" and a paper-and-pencil noninteractive test comprised of focused troubleshooting scenarios.

> Collectively, these results support the claim that SHERLOCK was effective in teaching avionics troubleshooting via its coached practice environment, where the rate of acquiring troubleshooting experience was consequentially accelerated. (Gott & Kieras, 1989, p. 70)

SHERLOCK differs from QUEST in several respects. In SHERLOCK neither the device nor the diagnostic expertise is simulated. It does not tutor an understanding of a qualitative model of the reasoning process of troubleshooting. Instead, considerable effort was spent on the development of a fully functional set of control

---

Add-Ten(number, row, column) Takes the number in a row and a column and replaces it with that number plus ten.

Decrement(number, row, column) Takes the number in a row and column and replaces it with that number minus one.

Find-Difference(number1, number2, column) Takes the two numbers in the same column and writes the difference of the two as the result for that column.

Find-Top(column) Takes a number from the top row of column and writes that number as the result of that column.

Shift-Column(column) Takes the column which is both focused on and being processed and shifts both focus of attention and processing to the column on its left.

Shift-Left(column) Takes the column which is focused on and shifts the focus of attention to the column on its left.

Figure 4.

Adapted from "Rules and principles in cognitive diagnosis," by P. Langley, J. Wogulis, and S. Ohlsson, in *Diagnostic Monitoring of Skill and Knowledge Acquisition*, Hillsdale, NJ: Lawrence Erlbaum Associates.

© 1987 by Lawrence Erlbaum Associates, Inc. Reprinted with permission.

panels (device models) and on the use of on-line schematic diagrams with high physical fidelity. The question of the utility of a problem space-graph in providing a basis for an adequate and flexible cognitive representation of the domain task remains to be answered. The flexibility and transferability of the the inputs and outputs from each system component distinguish whether the signal from the component is supplying power or information.

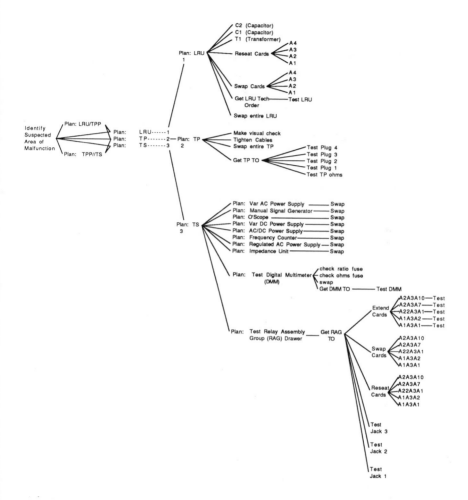

Figure 5. Hierarchical effective problem space of plans and actions for a single Sherlock scenario.

SUMMARY

Three primary themes emerge from the review and analysis of these automated systems and research on teaching troubleshooting (and medical diagnosis). First, the acquisition of troubleshooting expertise is seen as evolving over time. The novice first evidences a shallow understanding of system behavior, a lack of understanding of energy flow or power, and a reliance on a set of fixed procedures to locate faults. Expertise evolves with the development and use of a mental model of the system that represents the functional and structural properties of the device, a set of heuristics for fault isolation, and executive control strategies for monitoring and evaluating the effectiveness of these strategies or plans for troubleshooting.

Second, each of these systems shares the characteristic of having its architecture guided by a cognitive modeling of the the task. This cognitive modeling has provided a expert performance model of the task where expertise is decomposed into processes, heuristics, and strategies for problem solving. The modeling of the cognitive aspects of the task has enabled the developers of these systems to make explicit the connections between knowledge and skills. In this model, expertise is made explicit, observable, and therefore, trainable. In the instances where the automated instructional system has a diagnostic component, cognitive modeling techniques are used to identify misconceptions or "bugs" that students are likely to acquire while learning to perform a task. These anticipated student errors are then

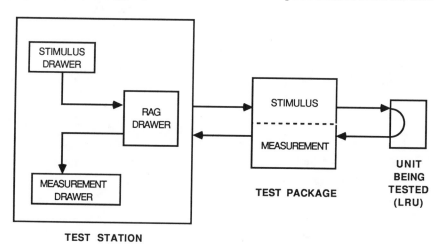

Figure 6. Top-level device model for avionics equipment configuration.

Figure 7a.

(1) The basic "Start Actions" menu (shown earlier in Figure 16) initiates the interaction and takes the trainee through preliminary set up procedures whereby the Unit and Test Package are hooked up to the Test Station so that the series of electronic tests can be run.

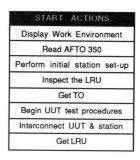

Figure 16a. Start Actions Menu

(2) Once a test in the series fails, a top level menu of plans is available to begin the fault isolation stage of the process. The trainee is presented the plan options that comprise the first level of the hierarchy in Figure 14. These options in effect split the complete equipment space into Unit vs Test Package vs Test Station or Unit vs a Test Package/Test Station composite (Table 11).

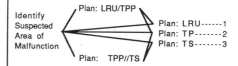

Figure 14a. Plan level of Effective Problem Space (EPS)

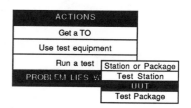

Table 11. Menu of Plans

(3) To illustrate the content and pedagogy of the hint structure, suppose the technician adopted a plan to investigate the Unit and took the action "Swap entire LRU" (Figure 14b) but needed help interpreting the outcome of the swap and in deciding what to do next. Table 12 illustrates the hints available for that situation.

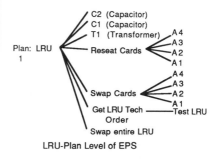

LRU-Plan Level of EPS

Figure 7b.

Exemplar Hint for Option after Swap LRU

Option (Level 5): Your initial thinking was the unit was bad. That was a good choice because the unit was sent to the shop for repair. The TO (technical order) states that the UUT Shutdown Command Output may be bad. Because you swapped the unit, we learned that the unit is good for this test, so there must be a problem in the Test Package or the Test Station.

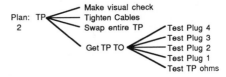

Figure 14c. TP-Plan Level of EPS

(4) Further suppose the trainee next suspects the Test Package. Table 13 illustrates three available levels of hints at the Test Package Plan stage (Figure 14c). Notice that this series of hints establishes the fundamental mental model of an electronic test in reasonably abstract terms by explaining stimulus signals and pathways.

Table 13. Hints for TP Plan

Level 2: The Test Package provides a path for Test Station Stimulus signals to get to the Unit and provides a path for the UUT signals to get the Test Station.

Level 3: An expert might test at the P2 plug of the Test Package to see if there is a Unit response signal getting through the Test Package. Remember, the response signal that this test is looking for is the Shutdown Command (25HZ) Output. If there is no unit response signal, then there may be a problem with the unit or a stimulus signal to the unit.

Level 4: The Test Package provides a path for Test Station Stimulus signals to get to the Unit and provides a path for the Unit signals to get to the Test Station. Is there anything different between this TO Test Step and the previous Test Step?

Figure 7c.

(5) Now, suppose the trainee moves to the most complex layers of the plan/actions hierarchy, the Test Station (Figure 14d). The Test Station Plan hints in Table 14 illustrate the range in the levels of abstraction at which explanations are provided. The Level 2 hint establishes the two major functional areas of the Test Station (Stimulus and Measurement), whereas the Level 3 series provides the exact steps for testing the Stimulus functional area.

Hints for Test Station Plan

Level 2: The TS provides stimuli to the unit and measures the unit's response signals. If either one of these functional areas (Stimulus or Measurement) goes bad, then the test will fail.

Level 3: If the Measurement functional area of the Test Station checks good, then you might suspect the problem to be in the Stimulus functional area of the Test Station. To test this area you must:

a. Review the TO Step to determine which stimuli are being sent to the Unit (this may involve looking at previous test steps for stimuli already set up but not cleared);

b. Trace (in the schematics) the identified stimuli signals to the output connector of the RAG Drawer;

c. Test each stimulus signal to ensure that it is leaving the RAG Drawer;

d. If a stimulus signal is missing at the RAG Drawer output, then trace the missing signal back to the appropriate Stimulus Drawer and test the signal path until you discover where the path is faulty.

Figure 7d.

(6) Finally, to illustrate how the fault isolation process is concluded, suppose the technician pursues the Stimullus functional area, tests the RAG drawer output as directed in Table 14, and traces the missing signal back to the activated Stimulus Drawer. The hints for testing the Manual Signal Generator (appropriate Stimulus Drawer) are shown in Table 15.

Hints for Testing Manual Signal Generator

Action (Level 5): The Manual Signal Generator should be sending a 25HZ signal to the RAG Drawer. This signal should be entering the RAG Drawer at the Plug 6/Jack 6 connection, Pins S and T. Sherlock has disconnected P6 from J6 on the RAG Drawer so that you can not measure the input at P6 Pins S and T with the o'scope.

Outcome (Level 5): The signal at P6 Pins S and T is +5VDC, not 25HZ.

Conclude (Level 5): This signal at P6 Pins S and T is +5VDC. In the TO Test Step that is failing, you set up the Manual Signal Generator so that it would output 25HZ. The Manual Signal Generator seems to be sending a bad stimulus signal to the RAG Drawer.

Option (Level5): The output of the Manual Signal Generator Drawer is bad. Maybe you should swap this drawer.

Figure 7e. TS-Plan Level of EPS.

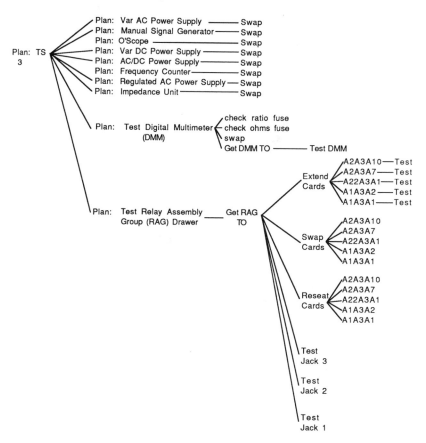

used to guide the development of instructional remediation of those errors. It is assumed that the trainees have the necessary prerequisite knowledge and skills, i.e., the global knowledge.

Each system provides an environment for the trainees to practice on troubleshooting problems. It appears that a fundamental understanding of theoretical principles, facts, and concepts is necessary for answering theoretical questions. Unless trainees are provided with instruction on how to use those fundamental understandings, however, such training is not sufficient for producing successful troubleshooting. None of the systems discussed in this chapter has implemented a formal cognitive theory of learning that is robust enough to teach general problem-solving skills. One reason for this state of affairs is the limited maturity of AI technology, e.g., representation of declarative knowledge is still very difficult to program in a computer language. The second reason is that most of the researchers engaged in this field are concerned with only one aspect of area of teaching (e.g., knowledge representation vs. natural language interface). Third, the building of these systems is very labor–intensive and requires a subject matter expert for each domain. Construction of systems that are flexible enough to teach in more than one domain therefore requires resources unavailable to many designers.

The third theme is that each of these systems was designed specifically for teaching troubleshooting in a specific situation or system and is based on an informal cognitive theory of troubleshooting (e.g., the use of a qualitative device model). These informal theories are neither general nor robust theories of learning, but rather are conceptualizations of the mental skills and knowledge that experts within a particular situation or system exhibit in performing troubleshooting activities. Likewise, they are not prescriptive with regard to training for the transfer of these problem-solving skills to other domains or to similar but different equipment. The exception is the work by Clancey and his students which separates specific domain knowledge from general problem-solving strategies. The importance of Clancey's model is that it describes the reasoning process in an abstracted way that is domain-independent and emphasizes the manner in which problem solvers use their system knowledge (of the physiology, anatomy, etc. of the human body) to develop situation–specific solutions.

As described previously, Clancey used this conceptualization in the design of his intelligent tutor GUIDON for teaching medical diagnosis. The model represented in the GUIDON system appears to be general enough to be used as a basis for a model in other problem-solving domains such as electronic troubleshooting. Similarly, in troubleshooting the technician must recognize malfunctions from their symptoms and select from a fixed set of methods one that is relevant to the specific situation. The other important feature of GUIDON is the use of heuristics rather that a fixed set of procedures (algorithms). This feature is not only important in medical diagnosis but is also required in troubleshooting where it is often infeasible to use an algorithm because of the uncertainty of the available information about the problem and/or the incompleteness of the technician's general model of the device (e.g., unknown system facts). The one feature lacking in Clancey's general model of problem solving is that of metacognitive processes, i.e., executive control, by which the student monitors and evaluates his or her progress and the effectiveness of the diagnostic strategy being implemented.

CONCLUSIONS

The evidence from the research on electronic troubleshooting suggest that to perform troubleshooting tasks technicians need to have both "how-it-works" knowledge and "what-it-is" (declarative) knowledge of the systems they are asked to maintain. Technicians need to understand the "how" and "what" of the device. It is our belief that these knowledges critically influence the use of procedures for troubleshooting. In addition to procedural and declarative knowledges technicians must also be taught functional and structural knowledge of the device and strategic knowledge within a context of use. Feigenbaum (1988) and Chi and Ceci (1987) have described the influence of the structure of knowledge and its interaction with cognitive processing. How knowledge is structured influences its accessibility, and how it is represented determines how it is understood and used in problem solving (Genter & Stevens, 1983; Greeno & Simon, 1988). Combined structural and functional descriptions of system operation have also been recommended by Psotka, Massey, and Mutter (1988) as part of effective explanations in intelligent tutoring systems. Moreover, the transfer of troubleshooting skills requires not only procedural, strategic, and device knowledge but also generic conceptual knowledge (Morris & Rouse, 1985; Swezey et al., 1988).

A pervasive theme in each of the chapters of this book has been an articulation of a theory of problem solving within a specific domain and then a speculation as to how or what might transfer from one domain to another. Unlike these other chapters related to academic disciplines such as biology, chemistry, and computer programming, however, we have focused on the real-world domain of troubleshooting in equipment maintenance. We have discussed the findings of empirical research on problem-solving skills from training studies, AI research on intelligent tutors, and studies of expertise in troubleshooting.

In attempting to formulate a unified theory of problem solving in the domain of diagnosis and troubleshooting we must first define what skills, knowledges, heuristics, and cognitive processes transfer from diagnosis and troubleshooting to other situations. Then we must determine how those skills transfer. In a narrow sense transfer can be defined as the effects of practicing diagnosis and troubleshooting on system A on learning or performing troubleshooting on a similar but different system B. Transfer occurs in one of three ways. Positive transfer occurs when practicing on system A improves learning or performance on system B; negative transfer occurs when practicing on system A interferes with learning or performance on system B; and no transfer occurs when practicing on one system has no effect on learning or performance on a second system.

The view of transfer that has guided this approach can be traced to the "identical elements" theory of transfer proposed by Thorndike and Woodworth (1901). This theory presumes that transfer will occur in situations in which identical elements exist in both the original and transfer situations. The degree and type of transfer that occurs will be determined by the *similarity* of the two situations. Generally, training studies driven by the identical elements theory take the following form: Two groups of subjects receive different training treatments and are given practice on system A. Then both groups are given practice and/or are tested on system B. The scores of the two groups on system A are compared in terms of amount, quality, or cost of learning or in terms of their performance of diagnosis and troubleshooting on system B. A frequent finding in experiments designed along this general form is that no differences in performance measures can be ascribed to practice or different training treatments. An often neglected aspect of this research is that the experimenters fail to specify *what* the "identical elements" are that are expected to transfer from one situation to another and *how* they should be expected to transfer. A general theory that accounts for transfer and that identifies transferable elements for the teaching of problem-solving skills has yet to be articulated.

Contemporary cognitive science has begun to address the issue of the nature of the elements of learning and problem solving that are expected to transfer. Based on their studies of expert programmers reported in this volume, Perkins, Schwartz, and Simmons address this issue. First they distinguish between "local" and "global" knowledge. Local knowledge consists of domain-specific schemata which are compiled in the expert and are often inaccessible. Global knowledge on the other hand cuts across several domains, is domain-independent, and is in the form of general principles, e.g., Newton's laws in physics or electronic circuit theory in troubleshooting.

In our studies of troubleshooting we have attempted to identify with some precision those elements (i.e., cognitive structures and processes) that might transfer from one troubleshooting situation to another. The elements that we think should transfer are the global knowledge of troubleshooting and the executive and self-regulatory processes sometimes called metacognition. Global knowledge of troubleshooting consists of generic troubleshooting strategies (such as "split-half" and techniques such as information flow diagrams) along with subject matter knowledge such as principles of electronic circuit theory and thermodynamics. It is our view that the representations of electronic or thermodynamic principles and laws are stored in the learner in the qualitative form of analogies or metaphors rather than in a quantitative form and that these qualitative models are used by experts to reason about system malfunctions.

The role of executive and self-regulatory processes in transfer has been discussed by Brown, Bransford, Ferrara, and Campione (1983) and by Sternberg

(1985a). In our clinical studies of expert troubleshooters (Wiggs & Perez, 1988) we found that one characteristic that sets expert troubleshooters apart from novices is that the experts spent more time than novices in the formulation of a plan of action for fault isolation and in monitoring the effectiveness of that plan. For example, the experts that we interviewed identified heuristics and strategies used in troubleshooting the electrical and hydraulic subsystems of a particular weapons system (the Improved Tow Vehicle). These experts reported that they applied these heuristics, strategies, planful behaviors, and self-monitoring processes in troubleshooting other systems such as the tank turret of an M1 tank as well.

In contrast, local knowledge is thought to be more brittle, more domain dependent, and less likely to transfer. In the domain of troubleshooting, local knowledge consists of the specific procedures for testing individual system components and test equipment and/or the functional and structural characteristics of specific system or subsystem components. For example, in our studies we taught trainees the specific procedures to be used to start up the Cummins diesel engine and the operational characteristics of the subcomponents of the fuel system (carburetor) of that engine. This knowledge did *not* generalize to the troubleshooting transfer task. Thus, these system–specific procedures or operational characteristics for the Cummins engine are not likely to generalize to the maintenance of other truck engines. Those more generic procedures involved in the use of tools such as wrenches, screwdrivers, voltmeters, and other common test equipment should transfer, however. In a series of experiments on troubleshooting, we have found that generic or conceptual knowledge of system components does indeed transfer from one situation to another.

Perkins et al. (this volume) have noted the inability of programming students to recall and apply specific programming procedures unless they were cued or prompted. They refer to this phenomenon as "inert knowledge." We have observed a similar phenomenon in trainees provided with general and domain-specific procedural knowledge who could demonstrate that knowledge on a paper-and-pencil test but were unable to use it in a troubleshooting task. These trainees were able to use this "inert" procedural knowledge on a subsequent transfer task, however. One explanation for the inability of our trainees to use this procedural knowledge in the initial task is that it wasn't until they were faced with a novel situation that the more general knowledge was advantageous because it provided a context for the use of the more specific knowledge. This explanation is consistent with Perkins et al.'s notion of the relationship between local and global knowledge.

Brown et al. (1983) and Perkins, Schwartz, and Simmons (this volume) have also demonstrated the role of monitoring and executive control processes in transfer. Sternberg (1985) has discussed the role of executive control processes as the basic process for transfer. According to this view trainees come to the transfer task with a set of strategies for troubleshooting, and it is only after some analysis that solvers select a candidate strategy based on their judgment of the similarity of the present task to previous tasks. They then carefully monitor and evaluate the progress of the selected strategy, making modifications as needed. Trainees must be explicitly taught these executive control and monitoring processes and must be given practice on their use in context.

In sum, we have presented the view that in order to teach general problem-solving skills we must understand how domain-dependent (local) knowledge and domain-independent (global) knowledge are to be combined with heuristics, executive control, and self-regulatory processes. The mechanism that we have suggested to account for transfer is the use of executive control strategies and metacognitive strategies. These strategies are used by trainees to analyze the situation and perceive the similarity between novel situations and past situations. On the basis of the perceived similarity between the two tasks, the solver then selects an appropriate plan of action for locating the malfunction, implements that plan, evaluates the effectiveness of the strategy, and selects an alternative plan or modifies the existing one as needed .

What remains an issue of concern for training not addressed by our research is that of the ontogeny of expertise and the development of the associated cognitive structures, particularly the development of skills that are transferable to other domains. Anderson (1983) has suggested that the acquisition of declarative knowledge gives rise to procedural knowledge, which becomes "automatic" or compiled knowledge with extended use. To date, however, few if any studies have supported Anderson's claim that declarative knowledge is acquired prior to and gives rise to procedural knowledge. In our most recent studies (Llaneras, Perez, & Swezey, in press), we have attempted to investigate the effects of order of knowledge presentation and have found that, for our experimental tasks, it matters little whether declarative or procedural knowledge is presented first. Knowing what knowledge is acquired first by experts and how that knowledge is acquired would provide us with a good idea of how to order and structure the content of training.

The views expressed are the author's and not necessarily those of the Army Research Institute, the Department of the Army, or the Department of Defense.

REFERENCES

Anderson, J. R. (1983). *The architecture of cognition.* Cambridge, MA: Harvard University Press.

Anderson, J. R. (1987). Skill acquisition: Compilation of weak-method solutions. *Psychological Review, 94,*192-210.

Baldwin, R. D. (1978). *Training the electronics maintenance technician* (HumRRO Professional Paper 7-78). Alexandria, VA: Human Resources Research Organization.

Brigham, F., & Laios, L. (1975). Operator performance in the control of a laboratory process plant. *Ergonomics, 26,* 669 - 686.

Brooke, J. B., & Duncan, K. D. (1981). Effects of system display format on performance in a fault location task. *Ergonomics, 24,* 175-189.

Brown, A. L., Bransford, J. D., Ferrara, R. A., & Campione, J. C. (1983). Learning, remembering and understanding. In J. H. Flavell & E. M. Markman (Eds.) *Handbook of child psychology* (Vol. 3, pp. 77-166). New York: Wiley.

Brown, J. S., & Burton, R. R. (1975). Multiple representations of knowledge for tutorial reasoning. In D. Bobrow & A. Collins (Eds.), *Representation and understanding: Studies in cognitive science.* New York: Academic.

Brown, J. S., & Burton, R. R. (1986). Reactive learning environments for teaching electronic troubleshooting. In W. B. Rouse (Ed.), *Advances in man-machine systems research.* Greenwich, CT: JAI Press.

Brown, J. S., & deKleer, J. (1984) A framework for a qualitative physics. *Proceedings of the Sixth Cognitive Science Society Conference* (pp.11-17). Los Altos, CA: Morgan Kaufman.

Burton, R. R., & Brown, J.S., (1979). An investigation of computer coaching for informal learning activities. *International Journal of Man–Machine Studies, 11,* 5 - 24.

Chi, M. T. H., Feltovich, P., & Glaser. R., (1981). Categorization and representation of physics problems by experts and novices. *Cognitive Science, 5,* 12-152.

Chi, M. T. H., & Ceci, S. J. (1987). Content knowledge: Its role, representation and restructuring in memory development. *Advances in Child Development and Behavior, 20,* 91-142.

Clancey, W. J. (1984). Methodology for building an intelligent tutoring system. In W. Kintsch, J. R. Miller, & P. G. Polson (Eds.), *Methods and tactics in cognitive science,* (pp. 51 - 83). Hillsdale, NJ: Lawrence Erlbaum Associates.

Clancey, W. J. (1986). Qualitative student models. *Annual Review of Computer Science, 1,* 381-450.

Clancey, W. J., & Letsinger, R. (1981). NEOMYCIN: Reconfiguring a rule-based expert system for application to teaching. *Proceedings of the Seventh International Joint Conference on Artificial Intelligence* (pp. 829-835). Los Altos, CA: Morgan Kaufman.

Crossmn, E. R. F. W., & Cooke, J.E., (1974). Manual control of slow response systems. In E. Edwards & F. P. Lees (Eds.), *The human operator in process control* (pp. 51 - 66). London: Taylor and Francis.

Duncan, K. D., & Shepherd, A. (1975). A simulator and training technique for diagnosing plant failures from control panels. *Ergonomics, 18,* 627-641.

Feurzeig, W., & Lukas, G. (1972). A programmable robot for teaching. *Proceedings of the World Congress on Cybernetics and Systems.* Norwood, NJ: Ablex.

Feurzeig, W., & Papert, S. (1968, May). *Programming languages as a conceptual framework for teaching mathematics.* Paper presented at the meeting, NATO Program Learning Research: Major Trends, Nice, France Publish DUNOD Paris, 1969

Feigenbaum, E. A. (1988). What hath Simon wrought? In D. Klahr & K. Kotovsky (Eds.), *Complex information processing: The impact of Herbert A. Simon,* (pp. 165 - 182). Hillsdale, NJ: Lawrence Erlbaum Associates.

Forbus, K. D. & Genter, D. (1986). Learning physical domains: Towards a theoretical framework. In R. M. Michalski, J. Crabonell, & T. Mitchell (Eds.) *Machine learning: An artificial approach* (Vol. 2, pp. 311-348). Los Altos, CA: Morgan Kaufmann.

Frese, M. (1989). Human computer interaction within an industrial psychology framework. *Applied Psychology: An International Review, 38*(1), 29-44.

Genter, D., & Stevens, A. L. (Eds.). (1983). *Mental models.* Hillsdale, NJ: Lawrence Erlbaum Associates.

Gitomer, D.H. (1984). *A cognitive analysis of a complex troubleshooting task.* Unpublished doctoral dissertation, University of Pittsburgh, Pittsburgh, PA.

Gitomer, D. H. (1988). Individual differences in technical troubleshooting. *Human Performance, 1*(2), 111-131.

Glaser, R. (1973). Educational psychology and education. *American Psychologist, 28,* 557-556.

Glaser, R. & Phillips, J. C. (1954). An analysis of proficiency for guided missile personnel: Patterns of troubleshooting behavior (Tech. Bull. 55-16). Washington, DC: American Institute for Research.

Glaser, R., & Bassok, M., (1989). Learning theory and the study of of instruction. *Annual Review of Psychology, 40,* 631 - 666. Palo Alto, CA: Annual Reviews.

Glaser, R., Lesgold, A., Lajoie, S., Eastman, R., Greenberg, L., Logan, D., Mangone, M., Weiner, A., Wolf, R., & Yengo, L. (1985). Cognitive task analysis to enhance technical skills training and assessment. (Contract No. F41689-83-C-0029). Brooks AFB, TX: AFHRL.

Goldbeck, R. A., Bernstein, B. B., Hillix, W. A., & Marx, M. H. (1957). Applications of split-half technique to problem–solving tasks. *Journal of Experimental Psychology, 53,* 330-338.

Gott, S.P. (1987, October). *Assessing technical expertise in today's work environment.* Paper presented at the ETS Invitational Conferences, New York.

Gott, S. P. (1989). Apprenticeship instruction for real-world tasks: The coordination of procedures, mental models, and strategies. In E. Z. Rothkopf (Ed.), *Review of Research in Education* (Vol. XV). Washington, D.C.: American Educational Research Association.

Gott, S. P., Bennett, W., & Gillet, A. (1986). Models of technical competence for intelligent tutoring systems. *Journal of Computer-Based Instruction, 13*(2), 43-46.

Gott, S. P., & Pokorny, R. (1987). The training of experts for high-tech work environments. *Proceedings of the Ninth Interservice/Industry Training Systems Conference* (pp. 184-190). Washington, DC: American Defense Preparedness Association.

Greeno, J.G., (1977). Process of understanding in problem solving. In N.J. Castellan, D.B. Pisoni, & G.R. Potts (Eds.), *Cognitive theory* (Vol. 2, pp. 43 - 83). Hillsdale, NJ: Lawrence Erlbaum Associates.

Greeno, J. G. (1978). A study of problem solving. In R. Glaser (Ed.), *Advances in Instructional Psychology* (Vol. 1, pp. 13-75). Hillsdale, NJ: Lawrence Erlbaum Associates.

Greeno, J. G., & Simon, H. (1988). Problem solving and reasoning. In R. C. Atkinson, R. Herrnstein, G. Lindzey, & R. D. Luce (Eds.), *Stevens' handbook of experimental psychology.* New York: Wiley.

Hamill, B. W. (1984). Psychological issues in the design of expert systems. (Report TR-ZEY-84-01) Laurel, MD: Milton S. Eisenhower Research Center.

Hart, A. (1986). *Knowledge acquisition for expert systems.* New York: McGraw-Hill.

Highland, R. W., Newman, S. E., & Waller, H. S. (1956). A descriptive study of electronic troubleshooting. In *Air Force engineering, personnel, and training research* (Tech. Rep. 56-8). Baltimore, MD: Air Research and Development Command.

Holland, J. D., Hutchins, E. L., McCandless, T. P., Rosenstein, M., & Weitzman, L. (1987). Graphic interface for simulation. In W. B. Rouse (Ed.), *Advances in man-machine systems research.* (Vol. 3, pp. 129-163). Greenwich, CT: JAI Press.

Johnson, W. B., & Rouse, W. B., (1982a). Analysis and classification of human errors in troubleshooting live aircraft power plants. IEEE Transactions on Systems, Man, and Cybernetics, SMC-12, pp. 389-393.

Johnson, W., & Rouse, W. (1982b). Training maintenance technicians for troubleshooting: Two experiments with computer simulations. *Human Factors*, *24*, 271-276.

Kieras, D.E. (1982). What people know about electronic devices: A descriptive study (Tech. Rep. No. 12 TR-82/ONR-12). Tucson, AZ: University of Arizona.

Kieras, D. E. (1987). What mental model should be taught: Choosing instructional content for complex engineering systems (Tech. Rep. No. 24 TR-87/ONR-24). Ann Arbor, MI: University of Michigan.

Kieras, D. E., & Bovair, S. (1984). The role of as mental model in learning to operate a device. *Cognitive Science*, *8*, 255-273.

Kurland, Y.J. & Tenney, L.C. (1988). The development of troubleshooting expertise in radar mechanics. In J. Psotka, L.D. Massey, & S.A. Mutter (Eds.), *Intelligent tutoring systems: Lessons learned*. Hillsdale, NJ: Lawrence Erlbaum Associates.

Laird, J., & Newell, A. (1983). *A universal weak method* (Tech. Rep. CMU-CS-83-141). Pittsburgh, PA: Carnegie-Mellon University.

Langley, P., Wogulis, J., & Ohlsson, S. (1987). Rules and principles in cognitive diagnosis. In N. Fredericksen (Ed.), *Diagnostic monitoring of skill and knowledge acquisition*. Hillsdale, NJ: Lawrence Erlbaum Associates.

Larkin, J. H., & Reif, F. (1976). Analysis and teaching of a general skill for studying scientific text. *Journal of Educational Psychology*, *68*(4), 431-440.

Lesgold, A. M., Lajoie, S., Bunzo, M., & Eggan, G. (in press). SHERLOCK: A coached practice environment for an electronics troubleshooting job. In J. Larkin, R. Chabay, & C. Scheftic (Eds.). *Computer assisted instruction and intelligent tutoring systems: Establishing communications and collaboration*. Hillsdale, NJ: Lawrence Erlbaum Associates.

Llaneras, R.E., Perez, R.S., & Sweeney, R.W. (in press). Effects of content sequencing and acquisition and transfer of troubleshooting performance. (Tech. Rep. No. SAIC-89-04-178). Maclean, VA.

Mayer, R. E. (1977). *Thinking and problem solving: An introduction to human cognition and learning*. Glenview, IL: Scott Foresman.

Mayer, R. E., Stiehl, J. G., & Greeno, J. G. (1972). Structural differences between learning outcomes produced by different instructional methods. *Journal of Educational Psychology*, *63*, 165-173.

McDonald, L. B., Waldrop, G. P., & White, V. T. (1983). Analysis of fidelity requirements for electronic equipment maintenance (Tech. Rep. NAVTRAEQUIPCEN 81-C-0065-1). Orlando, FL: Naval Training Equipment Center.

Miller, E. E. (1975). Instructional strategies using low-cost simulation for electronic maintenance (Tech. Rep. HumRRO-FR- WD- (TX) -75-20). Alexandria, VA: Human Resources Research Organization.

Morris, N., & Rouse, W. B. (1985). Review and evaluation of empirical research in troubleshooting. *Human Factors*, *27*, 503-530.

Moore, J. V., Saltz, E., & Hoehn, A. J. (1955) Improving equipment maintenance by means of a preplanning technique (Tech. Rep. AFTPTRC-TN-260). Lackland Air Force Base, TX: Air Force Personnel Training Research Center.

Newell, A., & Simon, H.A. (1972). *Human problem solving.* Englewood Cliffs, NJ: Prentice Hall.

Orlansky, J., & String, J. (1981). Cost effectiveness of maintenance simulators for military training (IDA Paper P-1568). Arlington, VA: Institute for Defense Analysis.

Papert, S. (1980). *Mindstorms: Children, computers, and powerful ideas.* New York: Basic.

Park, O. K., Perez, R. S., & Seidel, R. J. (1987). Intelligent CAI: Old wine in new bottles or a new vintage? In G. P. Kearsley (Ed.), *Artificial intelligence: Applications and methodology* (pp. 11-45). Reading, MA: Addison Wesley.

Perez, R. S., & Seidel, R. J. (1986). Cognitive theory of technical training. In T. G. Sticht, F. R. Chang, & S. Wood (Eds.), *Advances in reading/language research: Cognitive science and human resources management* (Vol. 4). Greenwich, CT: JAI Press

Psotka, J., Massey, L.D., & Mutter, S.A. (Eds.). (1988). *Intelligent tutoring systems: Lessons learned.* Hillsdale, NJ: Lawrence Erlbaum Associates.

Rouse, W. B. (1978a). Human problem solving performance in a fault diagnosis task. IEEE Transactions on Systems, Man, and Cybernetics, SMC-8. pp. 258-271.

Rouse, W. B. (1978b). A model of human decision making in fault diagnosis task. IEEE Transactions on Systems, Man, and Cybernetics, SMC-8, pp. 237-241.

Rouse, W. B. (1979a). A model of human decision making in fault diagnosis tasks that include feedback and redundancy. IEEE Transactions on Systems, Man, and Cybernetics, SMC-9, pp. 237-241.

Rouse, W. B. (1979b). Problem solving performance of first semester maintenance trainees in two fault diagnosis tasks. *Human Factors, 21,* 611-618.

Rouse, W. B. (1979c). Problem solving performance of maintenance trainees in fault diagnosis task. *Human Factors, 21,* 195-203.

Rouse, W. B. (1982). A mixed fidelity approach to technical training. *Journal of Educational Technology Systems, 11,* 103 - 105.

Rouse, W. B., & Rouse, S. H. (1982). Cognitive style as a correlate of human problem solving performance in fault diagnosis tasks. IEEE Transactions on Systems, Man, and Cybernetics, SMC-12, pp. 649-652.

Rouse, W. B., Rouse, S. H., & Pelligrino, S. J. (1980). A rule based model of human problem solving performance in fault diagnosis tasks. IEEE Transactions on Systems, Man, and Cybernetics, SMC-10, pp. 366-376.

Saltz, E., & Moore, J. V. (1953). A preliminary investigation of troubleshooting (Tech. Rep. No. 53-2). Lackland Air Force Base, TX: Human Resources Research Center.

Saupe, J. L. (1954). Troubleshooting electronic equipment: An empirical approach to the identification of certain requirements of a maintenance occupation (Doctoral Dissertation, University of Illinois, 1954). *Dissertation Abstracts International, 14,* 1966A.

Shortliffe, E. H. (1976). *Computer-based Medical Consultations: MYCIN.* New York: American Elsevier.

Simon, H.A. (1980). *Problem solving and education:.* In D. Tuma & F. Reif (Eds.), *Problem solving and education: Issues in teaching and research* (pp. 81 - 86). Hillsdale, NJ: Lawrence Erlbaum Associates.

Skinner, B.F. (1968). *The technology of teaching.* New York: Appleton-Century Crofts.

Smith, E. E., & Spoehr, K. T. (1985). Basic processes and individual differences in understanding and using instructions (Report No. 3029). Cambridge, MA: Bolt, Beranek & Newman Labs.

Smith, M.U., & Good, R. (1984). Problem solving and classical genetics: Successful versus unsuccessful performance. *Journal of Research in Science Teaching, 21,* 895 - 912.

Sternberg, R.J. (1985a). Componential analysis: A recipe. In D.K. Detterman (Ed.), *Current topics in human intelligence* (Vol. 1, pp. 179 - 201). Norwood, NJ: Ablex.
Sternberg, R.J. (1985b). Instrumental and componential approaches to the training of intelligence. In S. Chipman, J. Segal, & R. Glaser (Eds.), *Thinking and learning skills: Current research and open questions* (Vol. 2, pp. 215-243). Hillsdale, NJ: Lawrence Erlbaum Associates.
Swezey, W., Perez, R. S., & Allen, J. A. (1988). Effects of instructional delivery system and training parameter manipulations on electromechanical maintenance performance. *Human Factors, 30*(6), 751-762.
Tenney, L. C., & Kurland,Y. J. (1988). Issues in developing an intelligent tutor for a real-world domain: Training in radar mechanics. In J. Psotka, L. D. Massey, and S. A. Mutter (Eds.), *Intelligent tutoring systems: Lessons learned.* Hillsdale, NJ: Lawrence Erlbaum Associates.
Thorndike, E. L., & Woodworth, R. S. (1901). The influence of improvement in one mental function upon the efficiency of other functions. *Psychological Review, 8*, 247-261.
Voss, J. F., Blaise, J., Means, M. L., Greene,T.R., & Ahwesh, E. (1989). Informal reasoning and subject matter knowledge in the solving of economic problems by naive and novice individuals. In L.B. Resnick (Ed.). *Knowing, learning, and instruction: Essay in honor of Robert Glaser* (pp. 217 - 249). Hillsdale NJ: Lawrence Erlbaum Associates.
Wenger, E. (1987). *Artificial intelligence and tutoring systems: Computational approaches to the communication of knowledge.* Los Altos, CA: Morgan Kaufmann.
White, B. Y., & Frederiksen, J. R. (1985, July). QUEST: Qualitative understanding of electrical system troubleshooting. *ACM SIGART Newsletter*, pp. 34-37.
White, B. Y., & Frederiksen, J. R. (1986). Progressions of qualitative models as foundations for intelligent learning environments (BBN Report No. 6277). Cambridge, MA: BBN Laboratories.
White, B. Y., & Frederiksen, J. R. (1987). Causal model progressions as a foundation for intelligent learning environments. (BBN Report 6686). Cambridge, MA: BBN Laboratories.
Wiggs, C. L., & Perez, R. S. (1988). The use of knowledge acquisition in instructional design. *Computers in Human Behavior, 4*, 257-274.

Author Index

A

Abbott, V., 54, 64, 65
Ahwesh, E., 122, 153
Alibert, D., 83, 85, 87, 95
Allen, J. A., 120, 145, 153
Allen, R. D., 10, 18
Anderson, J. R., 56, 63, 71, 73, 74, 75, 86, 95, 97, 118, 148
Arocha, J. F., 8, 18, 38, 44

B

Baldwin, R. D., 117, 148
Bassok, M., 122, 150
Bee, N. V., 73, 96
Belenky, M. F., 80, 95
Bempechat, J., 80, 96
Bennett, W., 134
Bereiter, C., 48, 49, 64
Bernstein, B. B., 119, 150
Blaise, J., 122, 153
Blume, B. W., 56, 64
Bodner, G. M., iii, iv, 4, 8, 17, 23, 24, 30, 32
Bovair, S., 122, 151
Bowen, C., 8, 17
Boyle, C. F., 73, 74, 75, 86, 95
Bransford, J. D., 48, 49, 50, 64, 146, 147, 149
Briars, D. J., 72, 95
Brigham, F., 118, 148

Brooke, J. B., 119, 149
Brown, A. L., 146, 149
Brown, D., 109, 113
Brown, J. S., 70, 73, 75, 76, 88, 95, 96, 124, 128, 133, 149
Bundy, A., 72, 74, 95
Bunzo, M., 135, 151
Burdoff, C., 73, 97
Burton, R. R., 70, 95, 124, 133, 149
Bushey, B. B., 49, 65
Butler, M., 75, 97

C

Campbell, G. J. M., 37, 44
Campione, J. C., 146, 147, 149
Carpenter, T. P., 72, 73, 74, 83, 85, 86, 87, 95, 96
Carraher, D. W., 75, 87, 96
Carraher, T. N., 75, 87, 96
Carroll, L, 21, 22, 32
Carruth, G., 22, 32
Carter, C. S., 8, 17, 23, 24, 29, 31, 32
Carver, S. M., 56, 64
Case, R, 25, 32
Cassels, J. R. T., 8, 17
Ceci, S.J., 145, 149
Chaiklin, S., 71, 96
Champagne, A., 101, 104, 113
Charness, N., 36, 43
Chase, W. G., 36, 37, 43, 46, 64

156

Chi, M. T. H., 10, 12, 17, 46, 64, 145, 149
Chiang, C.,74, 86, 95
Clancey, W. J., 125, 126, 127, 144, 145, 149
Clement, J., 46, 54, 55, 59, 64, 65, 67, 109, 111, 113
Clements, D. H., 56, 64
Clinchy, B. M., 80, 95
Collins, A., 12, 19, 75, 96
Collura, J., 6, 18
Cooke, J. E., 118, 149
Crossman, E. R. F. W., 118, 149
Crowe, C. M., 3, 19

D

Dalbey, J., 56
Davis, R. B., 4, 17
de la Rocha, P., 3, 18
deGroot, A. D., 10, 17, 36, 37, 43
deKleer, J., 128, 149
Dreyfus, H. L., 75, 96
Dreyfus, S. E., 75, 96
DuBoulay, B., 52, 64
Dufresne, R., 104, 113
Duncan, K. D., 118, 119, 149
Dweck, C., 80, 96

E

Eastman, R., 122, 134, 150
Eggan, G., 33, 134, 151
Ehrlich, E., 22, 32, 54, 55, 64
El-Banna, H., 23, 32
Elstein, A. S., 37, 43
Ericsson, A., 35, 43
Estey, G., 55, 66

F

Falls, H., 11, 17
Farady, M., 47, 49, 55, 65, 66
Fawcett, H. P., 83, 84, 85, 87
Feigenbaum, E. A., 145, 149
Feightner, .W., 37, 44

Feltovich, P. J., 10, 12, 17
Fennema, E., 74, 83, 85, 87, 86, 95, 96
Ferrara, R. A., 146, 147, 149
Feurzeig, W., 56, 64, 133, 149
Feyerabend, P., 27, 32
Flexner, S. B., 22, 32
Flores, F., 75, 98
Forbus, K. D., 123, 149
Foss, C. L., 74, 86, 96
Frank, D. V., 31, 32
Franks, J. J., 48, 49, 50, 64
Fredriksen, C. H., 38, 43
Fredriksen, J. R., 122, 127, 128, 132, 153
Frese, M., 120, 149

G

Gabel, D.L., 8, 17
Gardner, W., 8, 18
Gelman, R., 88, 96
Gentner, D., 54, 59, 64, 65, 123, 145, 149, 150
Gerace, W., 104, 107, 113
Gillet, A., 134
Gitomer, D. H., 122, 134, 150
Glaser, R., 10, 12, 17, 46, 64, 117, 122, 134, 150
Goldbeck, R. A., 119, 150
Goldberger, N. R., 80, 95
Good, R., 10, 11, 13, 14, 122, 152
Gott, P., 120, 123, 134, 135, 150
Greenberg, L., 122, 134, 150
Greenbowe, T. J., 30, 32
Greene, T. R., 122, 153
Greeno, J. G., iv, 12, 35, 43, 70, 71, 72, 73, 74, 76, 88, 96, 97, 118, 121, 122, 145, 150, 151
Groen, G. J., iii, 8, 18, 23, 32, 36, 38, 41, 43, 44
Gullo, D. F., 56, 64
Gunstone, R., 101, 104, 113

H

Hall, R., 72, 97

Hamill, B. W., 123, 150
Hardiman, P., 104, 113,
Hart, A., 123, 150
Hayes, J. R., 3, 8, 12, 17, 18, 19, 22, 32
Hawkins, J. M., 22, 32
Heller, J. I., 12, 72, 73, 74, 97
Hendrix, J. R., 11, 19
Herrmann, D. J., 14, 19, 58, 66
Herron, J. D., 25, 30, 32
Highland, R. W., 117, 150
Hillix, W. A., 119, 150
Hinsley, D. A., 12, 18
Hoen, A. J., 117, 151
Hoffman, T. W., 3, 19
Holland, J. D., 124, 150
Holtzclaw, H. F., 26, 28, 32
Horwitz, P., 56, 64
Hotta, J. Y., 73, 97
Hutchins, E. L., 124, 150

J

Jacoby, L. L., 37, 44
Jenkins, M., 83, 85, 87, 96
Johnson, W. B., 118, 150
Johnson-Laird, P. N., 52, 65
Johnstone, A. H., 8, 17, 23, 32
Jungck, 12, 19

K

Karp, S. A., 11, 19
Keith, A., 83, 85, 87, 96
Kibler, D., 72, 97
Kieran, C., 41, 43
Kieras, D. E., 120, 122, 135, 151
Kintsch, W., 38, 72, 97
Kinzer, C. K., 50, 66
Kitcher P., 75, 97
Klahr, D, 56, 64
Klopfer, L., 101, 104, 113
Koedinger, K., 12, 19
Kruidenier, J., 55, 66
Kurland, D. M., 56, 65
Kurland, Y. J., 117, 122, 123, 151, 153

L

Laios, L., 118, 148
Laird, J., 133, 151
Lajoie, S., 122, 134, 135, 150, 151
Lampert, M., 83, 84, 85, 87, 97
Land, M. L., 56, 65
Landa, L. N., 5, 18
Langley, P., 134, 136, 151
Larkin, J. H., 12, 13, 18, 37, 44, 46, 47, 65, 72, 95, 122, 151
LaRussa, M. A., 23, 24, 32
Lave, J., 3, 18, 75, 87, 97
Leggett, E. L., 80, 96
Lesgold, A. M., 122, 134, 135, 150, 151
Letsinger, R., 126, 149
Lewis, M. W., 7196, 97
Leyden, M. G., 112, 113
Linn, M. C., 56, 64, 65
Llaneras, R. E., 148, 151
Lochead, J., iv, 6, 10, 12, 15, 18, 25, 32, 54, 55, 67
Loef, M., 74, 86, 95
Logan, D., 122, 134, 150

M

McArthur, D., 73, 97
McCandless, T. P., 124, 150
McDermott, J., 37, 43, 46, 65
McDonald, L. B., 117, 119, 151
McMillen, T. L. B., 30, 32
Mangone, M. E., 71, 96, 122, 134, 150
Martin, F., 47, 49, 65, 66
Marx, M. H., 119
Massey, L. D., 145, 152
Mawby, R., 56, 65
Mayer, R. E., v, 52, 65, 118, 122, 151
Means, M. L., 122, 153
Merriman, S., 56, 64
Mertens, T. R., 11, 19
Mestre, J., 104, 113
Miller, E. E., 119, 151
Moll, M. B., 10, 18
Moore, J. V., 117, 151

158

Morris, N., 117, 118, 120, 145, 151
Moser, J. M., 72, 73, 74, 96
Murray, T., 109, 114
Murtaugh, M., 3, 18
Mutter, S. A., 145, 152

N

Nebergall, W. H., 26, 28, 32
Nesher, P., 72, 73, 74, 97
Newell, A., 3, 11, 18, 35, 36, 40, 44, 70, 71, 97, 133, 134, 151
Newman, S. E., 75, 96, 117, 150
Nickerson, R., 56, 64
Niguidula, D., 51, 66
Norman, G. R., 37, 44

O

O'Shea, T., 71, 98
Ohlsson, S., 134, 136, 151
Oltman, P. K., 11, 19
Orlansky, J., 116, 152

P

Papert, S., 56, 65, 112, 114, 133, 152
Park, O. K., 125, 152
Pascual-Leone, J., 25, 32
Patel, V. L., iii, 8, 18, 23, 32, 36, 38, 43, 44
Pea, R. D., 52, 56, 65
Perez, R. S., i, iv, 120, 121, 125, 145, 147, 148, 151, 152, 153
Perkins, D. N., iii, iv, 10, 18, 47, 49, 51, 53, 55, 57, 63, 65, 66
Peter, O., 73, 97
Peterson, P. L., 74, 86, 95
Phillips, J. C., 117, 150
Pokorny, R., 123, 150
Polya, G., 14, 18, 26, 32, 75, 97
Pople, H. E., 12, 18
Popper, K. R., 1, 18
Psotka, J. L., 145, 152

R

Raskin, E., 11, 19
Rees, E., 46, 64
Reif, F., 14, 18, 122, 151
Riley, M. S., 72, 73, 74, 88, 96, 97
Robinson, W. R., 26, 28, 32
Rogoff, B., 8, 18
Rosenstein, M., 124, 150
Rouse, W. B., 117, 118, 119, 120, 145, 150, 151

S

Salomon, G., 51, 57, 63, 66
Saltz, E., 117, 151
Saupe, J. L., 117, 152
Saxe, G. B., 87, 97
Scardamalia, M., 25, 32, 48, 64, 66
Schliemann, A. D., 75, 87, 96
Schoenfeld, A. H., v, 10, 13, 14, 18, 19, 59, 66, 75, 83, 85, 87, 97
Schultz, K., 109, 114
Schwartz, S. H., iii, iv, 10, 18, 51, 55, 66, 73, 97, 146, 147
Scribner, S., 87, 97
Seidel, R. J., 121, 125, 152
Shalin, V., 73, 96
Shepherd, A., 118, 149
Sherwood, R. D., 8, 17, 48, 49, 50, 64
Shortliffe, E. H., 125, 152
Shulman, L. S., 37, 43
Simmons, R., iii, iv, 10, 18, 51, 55, 65, 66
Simon, D. P., 37, 44, 46, 65
Simon, H. A., 3, 8, 10, 11, 12, 18, 19, 35, 36, 37, 40, 44, 46, 64, 65, 68, 69, 97, 122, 134, 145, 152
Simon, M. A., 104, 114
Skinner, B. F., 133, 152
Sleeman, D., 71, 97
Smith, B. C., 76, 97
Smith, E. E., 122, 152
Smith, M. U., 4, 6, 10, 11, 13, 14, 17, 19, 22, 23, 33, 122, 152

Smith, S., 75, 97
Soloway, E., 54, 55, 64, 67
Spoehr, K. T., 122, 152
Sprafka, S. A., 37, 43
Stasz, C., 73, 97
Stein, B., 48, 64
Sternberg, R. J., 146, 147, 152, 153
Stevens, A. L., 52, 145, 150
Stewart, J., 12, 19
Stiehl, J. G., 118, 151
Streibel, M. J., 12, 19
String, J., 116, 152
Suchman, L., 75, 98
Swezey, W., 120, 145, 148, 151, 153

T

Tarule, J. M., 80, 95
Tenney, L. C., 117, 122, 123, 151, 153
Thompson, P. W., 73, 86, 98
Thorndike, E. L., 146, 153
Touger, J., 104, 113
Toulmin, S., 75, 98
Truxaw, C., 72, 97
Turchin, V. F., 2, 19
Turner, S. V., 56, 65

V

VanLehn, K., 71, 98
Vergnaud, G., 72, 73, 74, 98
Villa, E., 55
Vitolo, T. M., 73, 96
Voss, B., 11, 19
Voss, F., 122, 153
Vye, N. J., 48, 49, 50, 64

W

Waldrop, G. P., 117, 119, 151
Walker, R. A., 11, 19
Wallas, G., 14, 19
Waller, H. S., 117, 150
Weiner, A., 122, 134, 150
Weitzman, L., 124, 150
Wenger, E., 72, 97, 132, 153

Wheatley, G., 22, 27, 33
White, B. Y., 122, 127, 128, 132, 153
White, V. T., 117, 119, 151
Wiggs, C. L., 122, 147, 153
Winograd, T., 75, 98
Witkin, H. A., 11, 19
Wogulis, J., 32, 136, 151
Wolf, R., 122, 134, 150
Woodruff, E., 48, 66
Woodworth, R. S., 146, 153
Woods, D. R., 3, 19
Wortman, P. M., 12, 19
Wright, J. D., 3, 19

Y

Yengo, L., 122, 134, 150
Yost, G., 73, 74, 75, 86, 95
Young, R. M., 71, 98

Z

Zuboff, S., 75, 98

Subject Index

A

Abstraction reflechissant, 42
Algebraland, 74, 86, 96
Algorithms, 2, 6, 14, 18, 22, 23, 24, 29, 32, 116
Analogies, 103, 109, 110
Artificial intelligence, 36, 115, 123
Assumptions, 124
Avionics, 122

B

Black boxes, 133
Bugs, 138

C

Checks, 120
Chess, 122
Chunk, 16, 38, 120
Circuit, 124
    Electronic, 127
Classification, 126
Coaching, 132
Cognitive adaptiveness, 128
Cognitive analyses of problem solving, 74
Cognitive Modelling, 142
Cognitive Psychology, 35, 37, 40, 121
Cognitive Research, 87
Cognitive Science, 40, 69, 115
Cognitive Structures and processes, 87
Cognitive Task analysis, 122
Complexity, 119
Computational learning environments, 72
Computational tutor, 86
Computer programming, 46
Conceptual bridging, 110
Cummins diesel engine, 149

D

Debugging, 132
Diagrams, 103, 106, 142
Diesel engine, 120
Dig-out access, 49
Discovery learning techniques, 37
Domain-independent, 126

E

Economics, 122
Electromechanical troubleshooting, 113
Entity theorists, 80
Errors, 120, 132
Executive control, 121
Experience, 13

Expertise, 36, 39, 124
Expert, 2, 3, 10, 11, 13, 19, 101, 102, 122
  Models in intelligent tutoring systems, 73
  -Novice differences, 37, 103, 112
Explanation-based learning, 43
Explanations, 132
Explicitness, 136

F

F-15 fighter jet, 134
Fidelity, conceptual, 136
  Physical, 136
Flexibility, 117
Forward chaining, 36
Fractal concept of mind, 58
Fractal family, 60

G

General Problem Solver, 71
Geometry, 20
GUIDON, 125, 126, 127, 144

H

HERACLES, 126
Heuristics, 12, 36, 42, 71, 117, 121
  domain-specific, 13
Hierarchical, 122
Higher-level skills, 102
Hints, 132, 136
Hypotheses, 117
Hypothetico-deductive
  approaches, 37

I

Images, 124
Inferencing, 126

Information, organizing, 72, 119
  Processing, 69, 70, 75, 85, 94, 121
Integration, 131
Intelligent tutor, 40, 72, 125
Intermediates, 38

K

Knowing, 80
Knowledge, access, 48
  As design, 53
  Brittle, 149
  Compiled, 150
  Declarative, 118
  Domain-specific, 15, 105
  Engineering, 122
  General and local, 15, 46
  Global, 145, 147
  Hierarchical structure of, 107
  Inert, 149
  Local, 147
  Prerequisite, 120
  Procedural, 118
  System, 122
  Tacit, 125

L

Linear functions, 89
LOGO, 133

M

M-1 Tank, 147
Malleable-trait theorists, 80
Mathematical cognition, 76
  Discourse, 83
Meta-rules, 121
Metacognition, 85, 121
Metacourse, 51
Metaphor, 122
Microworld, 129

Misconceptions, 130
Model, anarchistic, 30
  Device, 123
  Diagnostic, 125
  Mathematical,
  Mental, 51, 120
  Physical, 129
  Pre-contextualized, 52
  Qualitative, 125
  Quantitative, 123
  Situation-specific, 124
  Solving text problems, 70
  Stage, 26
Motivational value, 130
MYCIN, 125, 127

N

NEOMYCIN, 125, 126
Novices, 38, 101, 102, 120

P

Pathophysiology, 38
Piaget, 41, 130
Pop-up access, 4, 49
Practice, 131
Predictions, 129
Problem-based learning, 37
Problem
  Complexity of, 12
  Definition of, 3, 22
  Real world, 7
  Space, 11, 131
  Space-graph, 131
  Versus exercise, 23, 27
  Word, 72
Problem-solving Model construction,
  72
Problem, Archistic vs. anarchisitic
  approaches, 25
  Cognitive analyses of, 74

Definition of, 22
External factors affecting, 14
Factors affecting, 8
in Geometry, 71
Internal factors affecting, 15
Implications of anarchistic, 29
Procedure based, 70, 94
Routine vs. non-routine, 4
Skills, 113
Weaker procedures, 15
Process Control, 116
Processing demands, 117
Production rules, 71, 123
Properties, functional/structural, 140

Q

Qualitative methods, 105
  Reason, 122
  Versus quantitative, 103
QUEST, 127, 128, 132, 133, 136

R

Radar, 117
Reading, 120
Reasoning backward, 37, 40, 42, 43
  Forward, 15, 36, 39, 42, 43
  Less than expert, 38
Recall-inference analysis
Redescription, 12
Remediation, 144
Representations, 119, 144
  In learning environments, 73

S

Schemata, 71
Self-monitoring, 112, 121
Self-reflection, 114
Self-regulation, 119
SHERLOCK, 130, 134, 135, 136

Simulation, 122
Simulator, 122
Situation-inferencing engine,
SOAR, 35
Social studies, 120
SOPHIE, 124
STEAMER, 124, 125
Strategy, 115
  Metacognitive, 119
Structured objects and events, 77
Subexperts, 38
Symbolic notations and structures, 76

T

Task analytic techniques, 120
Teaching for transfer, 56
Thinking-aloud, 140
Training, proceduralized, 118
Transfer, 111, 113, 115, 118, 121,
  132, 144
  positive and negative, 145

U

Understanding abstractions, 122

W

Working memory, 117